WHEN WE ARE the FOREIGNERS
WHAT CHINESE THINK ABOUT WORKING WITH AMERICANS

ORLANDO R. KELM
JOHN N. DOGGETT
HAIPING TANG

DEDICATION

For our students from all over the world who have inspired us for decades! Thanks.

CONTENTS

Preface vii

Acknowledgments xi

1
Xiaoliu Li, You Are Awesome 1

2
Rocks and Locks 17

3
Chinese Cookbooks, A Little of This and That 33

4
What a Cool License Plate 51

5
Sorry, We Don't Have the Bandwidth 69

6
If You Make a Promise, Keep It 87

7
Wǒ huì shuō zhōngwén 103

8
Carpe Diem 121

List of Contributors 137

PREFACE

We cannot say the exact moment it happened, but for right now, China is cool. Business professionals in the West are keenly aware of the steady economic growth and potential for new investments in China. Literally, every time we return to Beijing there are new subway lines. Every time we return to Shanghai there are new airports, new bullet trains, and of course, more traffic! Beyond these two gigantic cities, there are scores of others that seem to transform overnight in the same way. Despite the fears associated with any bubbles that are about to burst, there is a rush to be part of China's transformation. Along the way, cultural differences between East and West constantly affect progress, create misunderstandings, and damage financial gains.

The object of this book is to take a look at some of these cultural issues, with the intent of helping people avoid some of their negative repercussions. *When We Are the Foreigners: What Chinese Think About Working with Americans* is a collection of eight short case scenarios from mainland China that were designed to help readers assess the cultural factors that come into play when North American business professionals work with those who are Chinese. In preparation for these cases, the authors interviewed CEOs and employees from dozens of companies in China. These interviews included people from multinational corporations to small local start-ups. They were asked to simply tell their story about their experiences in working with North Americans. The eight cases are based on a composite of actual experiences that these Chinese executives related. Given the potentially sensitive or private nature of these comments, the names and the locations in the cases have been changed, but the cases do represent their actual observations and stories.

The format of each chapter in this book is the same. The stories focus on American and Chinese interactions, while highlighting the cultural issues. This is not to say that the business aspects are not important, but our focus will be on the cross-cultural interactions. As such, readers will not see a lot of data or numbers with the cases. The tone is informal, but that does not mean that the issues are trivial. In fact, our experience confirms that the success between North Americans and Chinese is often more related to cultural issues than to purely business. A little humility, patience, spirit of team-building, appreciation for differences in geography and time, knowledge of holidays, and an attempt at learning some Mandarin all go a long way in the success of collaborative efforts. So, each chapter begins with the case scenario, telling the story from the perspective of the Chinese who work with the foreigners, the North Americans. Yes, North America, sometimes we are the foreigners!

After presenting the cultural vignette, each chapter contains comments from three American and three Chinese executives who offer their observations, examples, and recommendations about the case. In all, there are nearly thirty executives who provide insight from their experience in American-Chinese interactions. Their comments represent their personal opinions. As such, these comments vary in content. Sometimes the ideas coincide well with each other. Other times, their opinions actually contradict one another. The most important thing is that these observations represent real ideas from real people, all of which help to understand the cultural issues that come into play. We should also mention that these guest contributors present their own opinions, and not those of the companies that they work for. After the executive comments, each chapter has a few summary comments from the authors to put the cultural issue in context. Finally, there is an appendix with a brief biography of the executives who have contributed to the book. It bears mentioning that all of the scenarios work independently from one another, and they can be presented in any order.

One final note of preface, it may be appropriate to clarify that this book is not designed to present a complete model of cross-cultural communication. There are many books and thousands of resources that deal with the foundational concepts of business culture. Readers who are interested in these helpful models are encouraged to consult some of these excellent sources. Below is a list of some of those that we find most useful.

General References

Gesteland, Richard R. *Cross-Cultural Business Behavior: Marketing, Negotiating, and Managing Across Cultures.* 2nd ed. Handelsshojskolens Forlag: Copenhagen Business School Press, 2001.

Hall, Edward T. *The Silent Language.* Doubleday, NY: Anchor Press, 1959.

Hampden-Turner, Charles and Fons Trompenaars. *Building Cross-Cultural Competence: How to Create Wealth from Conflicting Values.* New Haven: Yale University Press, 2000.

————. *Riding the Waves of Culture: Understanding Diversity in Global Business.* New York: McGraw-Hill, 1997.

Hofstede, Geert H. and Gert Jan Hofstede. *Cultures and Organizations: Software for the Mind.* 2nd ed. New York: McGraw Hill, 2005.

————. *Culture's Consequences: Comparing Values, Behaviors, Institutions, and Organizations Across Nations.* 2nd ed. Thousand Oaks, CA: Sage Publications, 2001.

Lewis, Richard D. *When Cultures Collide: Managing Successfully Across Cultures.* London: Nicholas Brealey Publishing, 1999.

Victor, David A. *International Business Communication.* New York: HarperCollins Publishers, Inc., 1992.

ACKNOWLEDGMENTS

Our appreciation goes to a number of colleagues and friends who assisted in the development of this project. First of all, many CEOs and company employees in China, who were willing to share their experiences in working with North Americans, made this book possible. Wei Luo and Jesse Zhou were extremely helpful in setting up some of the initial interviews, especially in Shanghai, but also in Beijing. Ms. Shujun Mo (Peking University) was also very gracious with her time as she helped to secure contacts in Beijing. Since we have changed the names and locations of the actual case scenarios, we cannot thank these people directly; however, we would like to simply thank all of those who participated in the onsite interviews. We hope our interpretation of their feedback reflects and represents their true opinions on the issued discussed. Thanks go to Prof. Jeanette Chen (University of Texas) and Haidan Wong (University of Hawaii) for using early drafts of these scenarios with their students and for the feedback they provided. Professor Wong also assisted in making several contacts for us with a number of Chinese executives. The guest contributors who added their comments and recommendations to each chapter were fantastic. Their observations added a tone of realism to the book. To each, we owe our gratitude as well. Finally, we also thank the University of Texas CIBER (Center for International Business Education and Research) for their support, especially in assisting with technical expertise and travel support.

1

XIAOLIU LI, YOU ARE AWESOME

Company: Tracking Parcel Company (TPC)
Focus: Worldwide Freight Service, including shipping, tracking, overnight delivery, and freight forwarding
Cultural Conflict: American communication style includes open and direct praise, which conflicts with the more reserved and humble style of Chinese communication.

Introduction and Synopsis

Tracking Parcel Company (TPC) is a worldwide freight service, including overnight delivery of packages and freight forwarding. In this case, we will see the interaction between the American expatriate Dale Jorgensen and his Chinese human resources manager Xiaoliu Li. We first note the background and experience that Mr. Jorgensen has had prior to this assignment in China. As is frequently the case, companies send expats who have previous experience abroad rather than someone who has no prior exposure to foreign assignments. Twenty years of experience, including assignments in Europe and the Middle East, have helped prepare Mr. Jorgensen for his work in Mainland China. Next, we note how much Xiaoliu Li picks up on the way Americans talk, using superlatives, positive phrases, and direct praise, which seem out of place among Chinese. It is interesting to see, however, that she has tried to adopt this style in the way that she interacts with her coworkers. Finally, this story exemplifies some of the challenges that non-native English speakers confront when they deal in delicate exchanges in a language where proficiency is limited. In this instance, the delicate exchanges directly relate to the fact that sometimes people are quickly promoted into management positions, often based on English language skills more than expertise in their work. This case also shows the complex array of issues that confront managers who work in China. In this brief exchange, we see how Mr. Jorgensen needs to deal with communication styles, issues of loyalty, hiring and firing procedures, and issues related to translation and language.

Case Scenario

Dale Jorgensen has been assigned to China as the senior area supervisor at Tracking Parcel Company (TPC). As a worldwide package delivery company, TPC provides the daily delivery of packages, freight forwarding, supply chain services, and a host of other related services in over 150 countries. Mr. Jorgensen has over twenty years of experience in the package delivery industry, having worked most of that time as a business development manager. His first expat assignment was during the mid-1980s in Europe, where he helped build operations in Germany and Switzerland. Then in 2004, after a brief assignment in the Middle East, Mr. Jorgensen was asked to take over operations in Asia. For the past five years, he has been living in Shanghai, experiencing firsthand the explosive growth of China. The fact that Mr. Jorgensen has spent his whole career with TPC is not unusual. TPC has a general philosophy of promoting from within, and as such, they have a well-developed employee training program. Consequently, they have a small turnover rate and a workforce that maintains a loyalty to the company. Nor is it by coincidence that Mr. Jorgensen's present assignment was preceded by previous expat assignments in Europe and the Middle East. China has unique challenges for international business. Local Chinese employees of TPC are still relatively young and inexperienced. TPC believes that expats have an important role in bringing training and experience to China. At the same time, TPC also recognizes that China's unique growth and potential requires the services of experienced expats. Clearly, Mr. Jorgensen relies on his previous experience in Germany and in Jordan for his present assignment in Shanghai.

Recently, Mr. Jorgensen has been working closely with Xiaoliu Li, the human resources manager for TPC China. Upon entering her office, an aura of competence is immediately apparent. Young, pretty, polished, professional, and easy to engage in conversation, Xiaoliu Li gives the impression that she loves her job. In fact, Mr. Jorgensen usually introduces her to others by saying, "I'd like you to meet our highly competent human resources manager Xiaoliu Li." Almost sheepishly, she acknowledges the introduction, always noticing, however, how extraordinary it is to hear the words "highly competent" when making an introduction. Those types of phrases are, in fact, one of her observations about Americans. "You Americans think everything is great, wonderful, fantastic, amazing, cool, or awesome." Not only do Americans think everything is awesome; they also say so, using these terms in both casual and formal conversations. That style of speech and feedback seems out of place among Chinese. "Chinese aren't prone to use those types of words when describing people," observes Xiaoliu Li, "much less when directly talking to them." Basically, Mr. Jorgensen is oblivious to the effect of the way he uses vocabulary. To him, it's just a matter of having a positive attitude.

For several weeks, Mr. Jorgensen and Xiaoliu Li were struggling with a delicate situation regarding one of their area managers. They suspected, based on circumstantial evidence, that this area manager was sending false packages to himself, trying to make his sales figures look larger than they really were. There were probably some under-the-table payments going on, too. The problem was they didn't have any hard evidence, but there was plenty of circumstantial evidence, and it was time to confront the area manager about it. Xiaoliu Li knew that they would have to let him go, but they also wanted to proceed cautiously because of the concern of doing or saying something that would cause a labor dispute, a lawsuit, or some type of arbitration. During their discussions, both among themselves as well as directly with the area manager, Mr. Jorgensen continued to be positive, and from Xiaoliu Li's perspective, rather protective of the area manager. He even considered just transferring the area manager to another assignment. "Frankly," Xiaoliu Li observed, "Mr. Jorgensen was just being too nice." There is nothing wrong with being nice, but when you have to fire someone, nice cannot be the same thing as soft. As the situation grew more intense, both Mr. Jorgensen and Xiaoliu Li realized that they needed more information and asked to have direct face-to-face meetings with the area manager. Truth told, it was really hard to get accurate information because he denied everything. Not only did he deny everything, they found out that he had even conducted secret meetings away from his office with his staff, trying to bolster his position, gain loyalty from his team, and position things for his demands if needed.

It might be helpful to note that these meetings with the area manager, like all other management-level meetings at TPC China, were conducted in English. TPC policy specifies English as the official language of the company, although employees are allowed to use their native language freely among themselves as well. Since Mr. Jorgensen doesn't speak Chinese, all meetings with him are conducted in English. In general, this doesn't cause any problems, and indeed, the Chinese employees are supportive of the policy. In Xiaoliu Li's case, she has traveled now and again, but she has only lived in an English-speaking country for about six months. Still, her language skills are well developed. She speaks fluently and handles both professional and personal topics without a sense of limitation. In reference to these meetings with the area manager, however, Xiaoliu Li felt that the use of English was hindering her ability to gather accurate information, due to the delicate nature of the discussions and because the area manager was denying any wrongdoing. Trying to get someone to admit to wrongdoing, to resign, or be fired is a delicate matter. At one point, Xiaoliu Li asked Mr. Jorgensen if they could conduct the meetings in their native Chinese. In doing so, Xiaoliu Li was able to use the subtly and nuances of language that are too difficult to maneuver in a foreign language. This helped a lot, and finally, they were able to get the area manager to admit to his actions. At first, he demanded an extremely unreasonable package in exchange for his resignation, but in the end, they were able to negotiate a compromise. Mr. Jorgensen was amazed at Xiaoliu Li's ability to change the situation and find a resolution, as the situation had become ugly and was looking fairly hopeless.

Fortunately, this experience with the area manager was exceptional. In general, TPC China enjoys observable success in worker loyalty. TPC China also has a general policy of trying to promote from within, including an excellent and well-developed training program for their existing employees. The presence of expats who provide expertise and experience combines with an energetic, young workforce that is anxious to progress and enter into management positions. If there is a problem with the promotions from within, it stems from the small hierarchy. From her vantage point in human resources, Xiaoliu Li admits that some people are promoted too quickly. Although she appreciates the policy to promote from within, she has also seen that, at times, promotions are based on an employee's command of the English language, more than his or her ability in sales and a proven track record. It's easy to see how this would happen. If the American expats are able to communicate more easily with a given person, then that person is also considered more readily for promotions. The problem is sometimes the other local employees have a better sense of who is the most qualified person for the promotion. It creates a difficult situation for the person who gets promoted as well as a difficult situation for all of the other employees.

Not long ago, there was a case where a promotion was given to a person who, in reality, lacked the technical and administrative skills to take on the new position. The local Chinese did not trust her, and they didn't have any confidence in her abilities. There were concerns about her sales volume and performance. As human resources manager, Xiaoliu Li's challenge was to deal with the complaints. And where did the complaints come from? TPC has an employee hotline where any employee can anonymously call a 1-800 number to voice concerns or complain about work-related situations. A number of complaints about this sales manager came in via the hotline. There were accusations of unfair treatment, favoritism, and problems with sales performance, and the turnover rate in the department seemed unusually high. Xiaoliu Li reiterates, "I like the employee hotline, and I believe it provides people with an anonymous way of bringing issues to our attention." However, she also notes that in China, where people avoid open confrontations and avoid differing opinions with their superiors, the presence of the 1-800 hotline is just one more way for people to avoid conflict resolution. "Think about it," Xiaoliu Li adds, "it's already difficult for Chinese to confront problems directly, and we've provided them with another way of avoiding the resolution. In some ways, I wish that we could help promote the idea of resolving problems among people rather than just calling a 1-800 number and have someone else deal with the problem." In this instance, Xiaoliu Li has been able to work with this new sales manager, and she feels that, with time, things will get better. Maybe if she hadn't been promoted so quickly, none of these problems would have ever happened.

This is not to say that Xiaoliu Li doesn't appreciate the perspective and contribution of the American expats who work in China. Prior to her work with TPC, Xiaoliu Li worked for another company for ten years as the supply chain solution manager. (It was in 2006 when there was a merger and Xiaoliu Li became an employee of TPC.) At her previous position, Xiaoliu Li had an HR boss who was an American. "Even to this day, she sends me birthday wishes, and I have a weird double birthday—the official one on paper and the real date. This lady sends me cards on both days." This manager treats all of her employees that way. She also taught Xiaoliu Li the importance of life outside of the office. "She'd always ask about my family and children. Chinese generally don't talk like that at work." This American HR boss was not a paperwork person. She was much more human-focused. In discussing her, it is evident that Xiaoliu Li admires the way that this person balanced her professional and personal life. And she was the only one who ever reminded Xiaoliu Li of such things. "It's from her that I noticed that while Chinese wish material things for people, Americans wish people good luck, peace, and happiness," observed Xiaoliu Li. "So I've even tried to adopt this style myself. I do tell my employees when they are doing a good job. I try to praise them verbally for their accomplishments." Xiaoliu Li realizes that this is counterintuitive to her Chinese traditions, but she believes it is important to recognize people. Normally, of course, Chinese managers recognize people in others ways—buying lunch for the employees, bringing gifts from trips, etc. "We feel it in our hearts; we just don't say it out loud. On the other hand, you Americans are like Santa Claus, always giving verbal gifts."

You know, Dale Jorgensen was right, Xiaoliu Li is awesome!

Observations and Comments from American Experts

DAVID HOLLINGSWORTH
BUSINESS MANAGER, MANUFACTURING OPERATIONS

Not unlike the example given, the early years of our manufacturing experience in China began with expatriates filling the leadership positions. Overtime, these positions have been replaced with local leadership, each of whom are required to pass an English language aptitude test as a part of their employment. While this process of developing leadership within the country has taken several years, we now have an established base of leaders with the required technical and manufacturing experience to provide adequate strength such that the site can be self-sufficient in producing all leadership positions from within.

In addition to the development of leadership within the country, many of the developing leadership roles for the future also have opportunities to do a work assignment in the United States, providing not only a platform to improve their English skills, but also to help in understanding the company's business culture. This also strengthens the working relationship upon their return, as they have developed a network of contacts to assist them in resolving challenges in the workplace back home.

I have found, in moments of greatest challenge when working with my China-based work team, that perceived language barriers and cultural differences erode as we focus our efforts and synergy on resolving the problem and meeting the customers' expectations. Even though our cultures are incredibly different and my language strengths are not Mandarin, when I participate in resolving these challenges as a work team, the bond between them and us becomes "we."

In the example given, while culturally Xiaoliu Li may have been uncomfortable with the compliment "highly competent human resources manager" given by Dale Jorgensen, she had been exposed enough to the American culture through her six-month United States work assignment, including having had a previous American boss who she greatly respected, that she understood the cultural differences and was not bothered nor did it hinder her ability to work with Mr. Jorgensen.

Mr. Jorgensen also recognized through his many years of expatriate assignments that while the official workplace language was English, he needed to trust Xiaoliu Li when handling the very difficult problems with the manager and that it was completely acceptable for her to speak in her native tongue to the manager so that she could effectively reach closure.

From time to time, in calls with China, while our dialogue in the meeting is all conducted in English, they will ask for a moment to converse among themselves in their native tongue to provide a response to a question asked. On those occasions, I have never seen this as a deterrent or an issue.

ROBERT BERKI
LEAD SYSTEMS ENGINEER

For the past several years, I have been involved in the transfer of technology and quality systems into various manufacturing plants in China. I found the TPC scenario relevant and familiar because it illustrates several ways in which communication can be influenced by language and Chinese culture. In the United States, we get to the point, ask questions, state opinions, and offer praise or criticism openly. We focus on the project. Making it happen on time and under budget is all that really matters. When working in China, you have to realize that their number one goal is to maintain order. They try not to disagree in public, they won't embarrass someone in front of a group, they will never say they don't understand, they never put their superiors on the spot, praise and criticism are withheld to avoid envy and embarrassment, and they are always measured and polite. The project will get done, but in China, how it's done is just as important as getting it done.

As in the delivery company scenario, communication in English is widespread and often necessary, but you can't let it hold you back. Large meetings held in English are good for introductions, presenting an overall plan upon arrival, and summarizing at the end of a visit. During the working portion of a visit, I prefer to stimulate discussion within a smaller working group. I will often ask them to talk about a given problem and give me a recommendation. I take a walk, come back, and then let them tell me what they have come up with. I am never disappointed. If you insist on being involved in every conversation, you are only preventing effective communication. Private conversations are also useful, as individual workers will not want to be seen as contradicting or upstaging their bosses. Later, you can present their ideas to the group as questions. Again, let them discuss.

As a visitor, one must be careful of praise. It is not a good idea to praise anyone publicly, lest you risk offending others who may actually be more deserving of credit. It is easy to mistake someone with the best English as more talented or a better contributor, while the group knows it isn't so. You can undermine your own credibility this way as well as end up assigning someone a task they are not qualified to handle. Americans express praise quite readily, but the Chinese believe in actions. Actually, I don't see anything wrong with their system, and as we often say, actions speak louder than words, but verbal recognition can be an important form of encouragement. Some Chinese managers recognize this, but praise (or criticism) should be carried out one on one.

Asking about one's family is usually not done, and although it may be a nice touch for a Chinese supervisor to adopt this behavior, I would be careful asking personal questions as an outsider. Asking about someone's wife, for example, may seem rather strange in a culture where this is not usually done.

Working in China does present unique challenges in communication and understanding, but they are not insurmountable. Understanding how to go with the flow can be quite an advantage. I usually find that if I *let* things happen rather than try to *make* things happen, there will be a better end result. The Chinese are very clever, and I am rarely disappointed. It is, of course, great to have someone with stellar English and people skills act as translator and cultural liaison. In the study, it was the human resources manager that filled this role, and for this, she was considered "awesome." For me, working in China, and working within the Chinese cultural framework, is in itself quite awesome.

Amber Scorah
Podcast Host, Amber's Chinese Buffet

Having worked closely with Chinese people for over six years, I related to this scenario. I have found that the experience of foreigners working with Chinese, though at times perplexing and somewhat frustrating for both sides, is a mutually beneficial experience. I have never grown so much as a person as I did during my years in China. That being said, the scenario here strikes very close to home. Recently, I had a similar situation arise where a Chinese person I work with did not communicate a complex cultural issue to me. I felt we were not only coworkers, but friends, and that friendship gave me the assurance that my coworker would feel comfortable communicating any issues to me that may have been at hand. However, this was not the case. One day, out of the blue, he sent an e-mail saying that he was resigning. He said that although he felt I understood the Chinese culture better than any foreigner he had come across, there were some things he could not make me understand and left it at that. In spite of my repeated attempts to contact him to discuss the reason for his discomfort or to see if we could find a suitable resolution to the problem, he would not respond to my messages, and I never heard from him again.

It is for this reason that I really relate to the baffling situation that is discussed here. In these kinds of situations, I have found it best to try to take things to a very personal level by one-on-one conversation with the party involved. Perhaps, in my situation, doing this before a perceived problem arose would have aided in avoiding this kind of drastic action. No matter what culture we are from, everyone likes to be heard, and if you can create a safe, private environment and draw a person out with tactful questions, this can go a long way in encouraging the party to open up. At the same time, finding a common ground can help, too; perhaps if you can relate a matter to a similar experience you have had where you felt a certain way, this can also create an environment where the person can feel comfortable to share. I have found that this one-on-one style of communication—whether it be praise, or conflict resolution, or anything else—can be effective, as it takes away the pressure of the cultural group and reduces things to the core of the matter on a human-to-human level. Generally, all problems come down to human relationships and relations, and this is something that transcends cultural barriers. Basically, no matter what our culture, we all have the same needs, desires, and problems; my years in China taught me that under the layers of culture, we are, in fact, not that different after all.

Observations and Comments from Chinese Experts
QUAN (MICHAEL) ZHENG, 郑权
BEIJING BIZTRAVEL INTERNATIONAL TRAVEL SERVICE CO., PARTNER

Understanding and respecting cultural differences between Chinese and Americans is the first step in accomplishing effective communication. Chinese people are more reserved. When they need to express their opinions and feelings, they always tend to be more mild and indirect, and they try to avoid words with strong emotions. They will do anything for you, but they are embarrassed to say it directly, even among their most intimate family members. In China, being "frank" and "honest" is commendable, but they are often thought of as being "immature" and "young." So, in this case, even though Xiaoliu is very good at English, she needs to use a mild Chinese-style approach to solve this issue of firing someone properly. Here "rhetoric" is definitely a derogatory term, whether you use English or Chinese. Chinese people always believe that actions speak louder than words. Capable people don't have to promote themselves, because "gold is always shining." It is only the incapable who feel that the only way to get a promotion is by having a good relationship with the leaders. (Chinese people think it is flattering.) These kind of people will be looked down upon in the company. Therefore, it is not difficult to understand why most Chinese employees do not recognize those who get promotions only because of their great English and communication skills or because they communicate well with expats.

But the Americans who I have met are very different. They are willing to share their feelings with other people, and they never hesitate to praise others. They talk and do things more directly. They don't purposely hide their preferences. They are more straightforward in their way of talking and doing things. They don't purposely hide their likes and dislikes. In fact, many Chinese people also appreciate this kind of attitude, but they are not used to this way of communicating. This is related to their traditions and what Chinese people have been taught from the time when they were young. But, nowadays, young parents and schoolteachers are encouraged to give their children and students more praise and more positive feedback. Chinese people have also started to realize that the old-life philosophy, like the saying "good wine speaks for itself," needs to be changed. Chinese people increasingly recognize good actions combined with good talk. Still, there is less respect in China for what is said than for what is done.

I require my staff to use different ways of communicating with different clients. With the U.S. customers, you can be more direct, but with the domestic ones, you need to be more careful and avoid being too straightforward.

Jun Liao
Global Business Manager

American communication style, with open and direct praise, is good for breaking the ice and getting along with local employees initially. Later on, however, it's important for expats to adjust their communication style to the specific local context. Fairness in promotion is another important area that I would like to mention.

As discussed in the scenario, direct praise is not very common in traditional Chinese dialogue. Influenced by Confucius's philosophy, Chinese people value the big family. To a certain extent, Chinese people view the whole nation as a big family. It is no surprise that in Mandarin the word "nation" (国家 guójiā) is expressed as "nation family." And Chinese people value harmony among family members. Members are encouraged to sacrifice their individuality in order to get along with other family members. Consequently, people adapt humble and indirect communication styles. And they carry this style into their social contexts (i.e., their working relationships). Again, this is because Chinese think of society as a big family.

However, things have been changing. The majority of the younger generation has grown up, because of the birth-control policy in China, in a nuclear family. They have been raised as the center of attention, being taken care of by their parents and grandparents. There is less of a need to be humble to get along with other family members. Also influenced by Western culture, younger generation Chinese are more direct and outspoken. Direct praise is not rare anymore, although it is still less frequently heard in China. Therefore, American communication style is more welcome in China nowadays. People are people. We all like compliments.

Nevertheless, expats still need to adapt their communication style in tough scenarios, especially those like the situation discussed in this case. When English is deficient in communicating subtle legal and moral liabilities to local employees, expats should not shy away from letting the local managers lead such conversation in their native language.

Even more essential than communication style, I believe an expat needs to be fair. Although I agree that local employees are initially impressed, encouraged, and motivated by open and direct praise, in time they will get used to such compliments. But, at some point, they will start focusing on other aspects of the expat leadership, and one of those aspects is how fair the expat is. Fairness is a universal leadership quality. I can see where promotion based on language proficiency is an easy trap for an expat to fall into. However, my advice is he or she be aware of the perception of fairness.

My sense is it is actually OK for an expat to base promotions on language skills in situations where language issues have created a big communication gap in the company management. Even in those situations, however, the expat should first help the local leaders understand the effects of the communication gap. Give them time to work on possible solutions. Then if they cannot improve the situation, the expat can easily justify the promotion of employees based on language proficiency.

You know, thinking about it, Dale Jorgensen is awesome as well!

JULIA WU
DELL COMPUTER, SENIOR MANAGER IN WORLDWIDE PROCUREMENT

I'm a little surprised that Xiaoliu Li still reacted sheepishly when being introduced as "highly competent." I thought that she would have been used to the American style of talking, being that she has been working in an American company for years. Personally, I like the American way of recognizing people. It's very encouraging. In Chinese tradition, however, we normally don't give verbal recognition to a subordinate. It's not because we don't recognize what they have done or that we're not willing to do it, but it would seem extraordinary to speak those good words in our native language. In some ways, it looks like these words are all reserved for written language rather than for oral communication. We all agree it's important to recognize employees publicly, so we have found a mutual way—by "speaking English." It's more comfortable to tell an employee "awesome, great job, fantastic" in English than it is in Chinese. Another common way to do this is to send recognition via e-mail to a large audience.

The promotion issue at TPC that is mentioned in this case is not restricted to American companies in China, but it is found everywhere, including in local Chinese companies. The person who has better communication skills with his or her manager will find it easier to get promoted. If this happens in an American company, it looks like the person who can speak English better will get promoted easier. To me, however, this shouldn't be an issue. In American companies, everything is related to getting results. Communication is just one of the areas where we evaluate a manager's performance. However, business results, direct staff turnover rates, etc. will also weigh heavily in their performance evaluation.

Agreed, it is difficult to fire an employee without causing a dispute and without the fear of a lawsuit. China has recently published a new version of the labor laws, which are very protective of the employee. From my own experience, I remember, about ten years ago, when I was working at my previous job in a manufactory in Shenzhen. I had been at this position for about a month, and my predecessor told me that one member of our staff was a low performer and had been difficult to manage. One day, she didn't follow my instructions, and she challenged my leadership in front of my staff. I then told her to go to the finance department to pick up her salary and to leave immediately. In China, we call this "杀鸡敬猴," and I know that it would be almost impossible to be able to do that as easily nowadays. Today's Chinese workforce is more knowledgeable about how to utilize labor laws to protect themselves. In fact, I really admire what Xiaoliu Li did to handle the area manager's situation. To be able to find a solution to this problem and to have him turn in his resignation by himself was impressive. This shows that she can manage people using her strong interpersonal communication skills as well as strong situational negotiation skills.

Note: 杀鸡敬猴 = *shā jī jìng hóu*

This literally means "kill chickens to scare monkeys," which refers to punishing someone so that others will not make the same mistake.

Observations and Comments from the Authors

This scenario exemplifies a number of interesting cultural issues that come up between North Americans and Chinese. First, experts who study cross-cultural issues often note that the way people receive and give compliments is culturally based. North Americans are typically direct in the praise that is given, but they also respond to praise by giving somebody else the credit. For example, the compliment "Your dress is very pretty" may incur a response such as "Thank you, I bought it at Macy's." In other words, the dress is pretty because Macy's sells pretty dresses. It makes people sound less arrogant when the compliment is diverted to another. Rather than diverting the compliment, Asian cultures often negate a compliment. When told that a dress is pretty, a Chinese person may say something like, "No, it really isn't a very pretty dress." North Americans think this is a strange response to a compliment, but it happens all the time. This is one of the reasons why Xiaoliu Li had to get used to the direct compliments that Dale Jorgensen gave to her. Chinese are also more sensitive about giving compliments because a compliment to one person, highlighting that person, may mean that another deserving person does not get a compliment. Rather than confront that possibility, it is easier to not give the compliment.

It is also significant to note that Mr. Jorgensen was very direct in his oral praise. Notice that he thought of phrases like "You are great" and "You are awesome" as simple ways to show a positive attitude. Chinese are more reserved in this sense. This is what experts refer to as "affect display," or how much we reveal our emotions. An angry person in one culture may be just as angry as another person from a different culture, but he or she may not demonstrate that anger as openly. A happy person in China may be as happy as a person in Texas, but he or she may not show it as openly. The mistake that is made is to assume that people show their emotions equally. Just because it is displayed differently does not mean that the other person does not have the same emotions.

This case scenario also effectively demonstrates the limitations that come when using English as a non-native language. Native speakers of English seldom appreciate the amazing ability that they have to soften their words, make subtle changes in meaning, and adjust their tone. These changes require high levels of proficiency. When Xiaoliu Li asked to speak to the dishonest area manager in Mandarin, she was returning to the ability to use those kinds of subtleties. The lesson here is to be sensitive to the fact that if the whole world is trying to communicate with North Americans in English, give them a break by not holding them to the same standards of subtlety that are part of a native speaker's abilities. People are going to come across sounding overly blunt, but sometimes, it is simply because their language skills are limited. This scenario also demonstrated some nice examples of how authority is perceived, based on how people were promoted at TPC. North Americans begin from an assumption that all people are basically equal. Consequently, power and authority can be transferred, exchanged, bestowed, and taken away quite easily. For the Chinese, more deference is given to those who have authority, which seldom would be casually passed on from one person to another. Knowing this, we can better appreciate how significant it would be if someone were to receive a promotion because of English language proficiency rather than because of more salient job-related abilities. Our recommendation is that North Americans be sensitive to the ramifications that come from the casual exchange of authority.

For those who want to use the book as a way to talk to others about these cultural issues, here are some possible topics and questions for discussion:

1. David Hollingsworth talks about the development of Chinese employees. Some have been given temporary assignments in the United States, while others have been promoted over time in China. Gradually, the leadership becomes localized. Discuss the potential advantages and disadvantages of this from both the Chinese and American perspective.

2. Comment on David Hollingsworth's interesting observation that cultural differences erode as they focus on the resolving customers' expectations and problems.

3. Note that Julia Wu observes that verbal praise would seem out of place when speaking in her native Chinese, but somehow this is more easily spoken when talking in English. What does this tell us about using native and non-native languages?

4. Thinking of Julia Wu's experience about ten years ago when she fired an employee compared to the current situation of new labor laws, what does this indicate to Americans who work with the Chinese workforce.

5. Try to identify some of the words and phrases that Americans use that might seem extreme to Chinese. Wow, I bet you are really great at identifying them! How might these affect communication?

6. What suggestions can you think of to respond to the problem of hiring people too quickly? If the available pool is small and promotions are needed, what can you do?

2

ROCKS AND LOCKS

Company: Lock-It-Up
Focus: Manufacturer and supplier of architectural hardware, especially locks
Cultural Conflict: Chinese communication style involves providing context, where Americans directly focus on the target. As a result, one seems evasive and the other seems blunt.

Introduction and Synopsis

High quality comes at a price. Of course, China is developing in terms of the concept of quality, but the issue in this case is not just about quality and price, but how those issues are communicated between the Chinese and the Americans. Hong Zhuang is the general manager of Lock-It-Up China, a manufacturer and supplier of locks and security products. His main challenge in Shanghai is convincing his Chinese clients that they should pay a little more for quality. The main challenge with his American partners is getting them to understand why the Chinese do not want to pay more. Behind all of this, in terms of communication, is the fact that the Chinese depend on context, while Americans are target-focused. Hong Zhuang is stuck in the middle. Interestingly enough, in this case, we also see how positively the Chinese react when the Americans come for site visits. Not only do they meet with the executives, but they also spend time with the distributors and end-users. Of course, from the American perspective, this is done to gather better information about how their product is being used. Ironically, from the Chinese perspective, they appreciate the personal attention and recognition. Without even knowing it, the Americans are providing context.

Case Scenario

Hong Zhuang is the general manager of Lock-It-Up China, a leading manufacturer and supplier of architectural hardware, particularly in the lock industry. Especially in cities like Shanghai, where construction is king and where cranes have been affectionately called the national bird of China, it is no wonder that Lock-It-Up China enjoys much success with their security products (like door locks). Just think of all of the locks on every door of every high-rise building that you see in Shanghai. From deadbolts to levers, from door handles to electronic security systems, it's got to be big business. Furthermore, Lock-It-Up represents Yale Locks, one the most respected names in high-quality security products.

Security and China—well, who would know more about security than the country that built the Forbidden City? Chances are an advertising agency would love to create a commercial that has moats, gates, and golden door nails on one hand and padlocks and mortise locks on the other. In fact, interestingly enough, the Forbidden City provides good background information to understand the case of Lock-It-Up China. If you ever visit the Forbidden City in Beijing, you will enter the Imperial Garden in the rear. And within the Imperial Garden there is a rock formation that is about twenty feet high with a small building at the top. In front of this formation is a sign that reminds visitors to stay off the rocks. In Chinese the sign says, "勿 因 一 时 疏 忽 破 坏 永 恒 美 好 (*wù yīn yì shí shū hū pò huài yǒng héng měi hǎo*)," and the English translation reads, "A single act of carelessness leads to the eternal loss of beauty." It's a pretty interesting translation because the Chinese words literally mean, "Don't because of temporary carelessness ruin eternal beauty." How does this relate to Lock-It-Up China? Notice how subtle the communication is. Where Chinese communication provides context and background without being overly blunt or direct, American communication style can be extremely concise and direct. The problem at hand for Hong Zhuang is the Americans he works with are less concerned about the context and background. To the Americans, the Lock-It-Up brand is of the highest quality. Within the lock industry, everyone knows that the American standard is even higher than the European. So, to them, this issue is simply that quality costs a little more. Frankly, they are not interested in all of the "little details." Consequently, Hong Zhuang has had a hard time convincing the Americans that their price is too high. "Their margin is very high, and it affects our ability to sell in China." Hong Zhuang explains that their mechanical locks that sell for 300 RMB per lock are about half that price among their competitors. The problem is Lock-It-Up has no product for the middle-range market.

Hong Zhuang has tried on many occasions to get the Americans to understand things from his Chinese perspective (providing the context). First, he tried to explain to them all the reasons whey they should lower the price, which they were not willing to do. Then he discussed possible reasons for wanting to manufacture the locks in China, which they also were not willing to do. Finally, Hong Zhuang asked if it would be possible to create a new product using the Lock-It-Up brand name to create a middle-range product, but again, they were unwilling to do so.

"I'm not sure why they don't want to do this. Maybe they are afraid of something. Maybe they are afraid that by creating a new product here in China they would hurt local production in the United States." Presently, almost all of the locks are made in the United States (except for some parts that come from Mexico). Lock-It-Up has a strong sense of "Made in USA," and chances are they do not want to jeopardize that. Hong Zhuang suspects that perhaps they are afraid it would cause them to close factories in the United States. Lock-It-Up, although international, is very much an American company. The CEO is American and about 40 percent of its business is in the United States. There is almost some irony here. For a group that values direct communication so highly, Hong Zhuang just can't figure out why Lock-It-Up isn't jumping at the opportunity to manufacture in China.

As opposed to being context-oriented, Americans are generally more what one calls target-oriented. As Hong Zhuang states, "In some ways, the Americans do not want to know about these issues. They give you a goal to reach, and they really aren't interested in the process details. They give us a goal—how many you will sell, how you will distribute, and how many sales you will have in a specific time." In other words,

"Here's the objective, you worry about the details." Hong Zhuang notes that whenever the Americans visit China, they are totally focused on these goals. (As an aside, he compares this to the Europeans who he believes are more focused on paperwork and reports. "The Europeans always want more reports!")

Hong Zhuang adds another example to show how target-focused the Americans are. Recently, an American manager (from a different company, not Lock-It-Up) wanted to hire a staff member in China. His company previously had their own office space in Shanghai, but it was not going well and was expensive. So they decided to let most of the local people go, and they closed the physical office. Anyway, the American manager asked Hong Zhuang if he could physically place his person in Hong Zhuang's office. Hong Zhuang calculated the cost to put this person in his office and gave him the price. But the American manager thought the price was too expensive. In the end, the company did retain this person, and he is located in Hong Zhuang's office. "I was happy to help out, but I was amazed to see how rigid the American manager's position was. He just wasn't willing to negotiate with me." Hong Zhuang sees this as another example of their being target-focused. The American wanted to close his Shanghai offices and retain this person in Hong Zhuang's office. His blunt and focused manner wouldn't even entertain any of the details, only the result.

On the positive end, there is a flip side to this direct approach. "When the Americans come to visit us, they really know how to create a friendly atmosphere." Hong Zhuang especially notes this as compared to the Europeans, who he believes just want to have formal meetings. Americans have more flexibility, which stems from the "customer is always right" attitude. "When Americans visit, not only do they have meetings with us in the office, but they always take time to visit with our distributors." The result is the distributors feel good because they get the special attention in front of the local managers and because the Americans want to know about their observations about the products. The sales executives also like this because they look good in front of the American visitors and in front of the distributors. Furthermore, Hong Zhuang adds that the Americans like to visit with the end-users of the products, too. Again, the end-users feel good because the Americans want to see how their locks are actually being used. Additionally, the distributors again look good in front of the end-users and in front the sales managers. "Truly, our American visitors do a great job of raising everyone's image with the complete line of visits. I've noticed that our European visitors spend more time in office visits going over the reports. They almost never take the time for site visits with distributors and end-users." It is interesting to note that the Americans conduct these visits in order to directly assess their products, but the by-product of these visits, from the Chinese perspective, is more in how it positively affects how the local people feel about their work. In other words, they see it as building context with the person.

So has there been any progress on getting the Americans to assess the problem of the high price of their locks? Not really. Hong Zhuang has been left with the same issue as always: Assess the goal and figure out the details. Too bad the Americans still don't understand "a single act of carelessness leads to the eternal loss of beauty."

Observations and Comments from American Experts
DAVID HOLLINGSWORTH
BUSINESS MANAGER, MANUFACTURING OPERATIONS

On one of my trips to China, I also had the opportunity to visit the Forbidden City. One of the managers from the factory used his personal time on a Saturday to show me this wonderful landmark. It was a most incredible experience. He spent hours explaining the symbolism and intricate detail of each part of the city. It was wonderful, as he not only showed me the city, but he added all the history, the detailed stories surrounding the walls, the statues, the locations of each building, and the meaning of the different colors used throughout the city. He brought the city to life for me. You might say that he provided the context of the city for me. This idea of context, however, is a potential cause for tension in the workplace.

That is to say, in a culture rich in context, it can be challenging for Chinese people to interact with a culture that is focused mostly on results. With any company, goals and the achievement of those goals is essential for survival. Neither culture would disagree with the need to achieve goals and to prioritize results; however, the communication surrounding goal setting and the monitoring of goal performance can create cultural challenges. By the nature of my job, I monitor goal performance nearly every day. I want to know if we are on plan to achieve our goals. If we are on plan, great, let's move on. If we are not, I want to see what actions are being taken to correct the drift. In my job, I need to know what happened that caused the miss so that I can ensure that it has been corrected. I am typically most interested in what has to be done to get back on plan.

I recall one occasion when the desired objective for the factory was not on plan, and the people at the factory wanted to provide the context to explain why. This was not a language barrier, but their cultural desire to provide the context was something that I interpreted as excuses and delays at getting to the root cause of the problem in order to be able to move forward to the resolution. In this specific example, fortunately, a third participant understood the difference in cultural accountability and provided a neutral position to lead both parties in to collaborative resolution instead of conflict resolution. Without this help, emotions could have easily flared, which would have destroyed trust and hindered collaboration.

In the Lock-It-Up example, it is important for both parties to understand that they share mutual goals and objectives. However, Hong Zhuang, in his efforts to provide context, is frustrated with the unwillingness of his American-based company to give him a chance. And his American-based managers are frustrated because they just want him to produce the results as requested. If the cultural differences in communication are not understood—and monitored—this could easily lead to mistrust and a loss of focus. Recognizing the differences and using them as an advantage rather than a conflict would greatly strengthen the position of the company. Hong better understands his culture, as such he is able to provide significant context in his market for the company's success. Hong also needs to understand that the American management team has been successful in their business model for many years, and they may shed significant insight into their methods and strategies. Combining the context from each side and agreeing on a consistent performance metric will allow both to mutually own the end results.

A.J. WARNER
MBATOUCHDOWN.COM, PRESIDENT

One of the major reasons why the Americans in the story visited their Chinese subsidiary and had meetings with their Chinese distributors was to find ways to expand the business. I feel from reading the interview that Hong Zhuang has many useful ideas to grow the business in China; however, cultural differences may have hindered his ability to effectively share these helpful thoughts with his American counterparts, such as the need for mid-priced products. I have found that although many Chinese staff members possess great ideas that would help, they often do not bring them up in key meetings. Too often Chinese staff members are hesitant to come forward with their suggestions, particularly when speaking in English. They may be worried about losing face if their idea is not 100 percent correct or accepted by the other team members.

The Chinese education may be a major reason for this dilemma. While the American education system encourages and rewards students for voicing their opinions, the Chinese education focuses on memorization and the reciting of knowledge. I have talked with many Chinese friends who told me stories of memorizing information word for word and, during an exam, being able to see the exact page of memorized information from a book in their mind. While interviewing college students, I have observed them reciting every answer from memory. As they spoke, I could see their eyes going left to right as if they were "reading" back what they memorized. Such examples of memorization are something I could never imagine an American doing. From my standpoint, the difference is a product of the unique Chinese education system. In the past, Chinese education did not encourage students to propose their own ideas. While this is changing in China's current education system, today's businesspeople are still influenced by their education twenty to thirty years ago that discouraged voicing opinions.

My recommendation for American businesspeople is to strongly encourage their Chinese counterparts and staff to voice their ideas and suggestions. Often, it takes many attempts to convince them to share their opinions and to help them know that, even if contrary, they will be warmly welcomed. The results from the company will be well worth the effort. Over time, Chinese staff will become more comfortable in sharing their deeper thoughts with their Americans counterparts, which is vital for the success of business in China. By not making enough effort to get Chinese to share their thoughts, a company will end up with this "loss of beauty." The bottom line is the American managers need to encourage their Chinese staff and business partners to share their actual thoughts about how to solve a problem or how to improve a service/product.

SANDOR WEISS
MILNER WEISS, MANAGING DIRECTOR

I can certainly sympathize with Hong Zhuang's dilemma. I am placed in similar circumstances in virtually all of my deals. Where my firm acts as financial advisor, our client is most often a Chinese company and the investors we speak with are American and/or European. I am forced to be the cultural mediator between the Chinese target company and the foreign investor. The skills required to perform this mediation successfully are even more important to my business than competence in corporate finance! In a typical private equity investment situation, the prevailing attitudes might be as follows:

American Investor: The prospective investor has very little patience for conversation before seeing a highly detailed information memorandum or prospectus and detailed financial information. They have only one goal in mind at the outset, and that is to analyze the facts and determine if a company visit and ensuing conversations are worth their time and money. The idea of meeting the owners and managers of the Chinese target company with very little detailed information in hand and no prior analysis is almost repugnant to them. It's almost as if you're wasting their time if you don't come calling with a fifty-page document and a detailed financial model in hand. They're not interested in context, just getting to the bottom line.

Chinese Target Company: The Chinese company owners and management are shocked at the suggestion that confidential information about their company should be compiled in a document and offered to complete strangers, even with a signed nondisclosure agreement. They want to know that a prospective investor is genuinely interested in becoming involved in their business and has the wherewithal to make an investment. In their minds, this entails significant personal interaction on both business and social levels. They would expect a visit from the prospective investors and a slow lead-in to more detailed business conversations. Socializing over a meal, and even karaoke, would be part of the visit. Only after everyone is comfortable that there is a real possibility of doing business together is detailed information brought forth.

The differences are usually confined to the initial stages of interaction as described. Once both sides are working together, ideas regarding due diligence and other details are not significantly different.

Fortunately, I usually have more success in mediating these situations than poor Hong Zhuang. In most cases, the Chinese company can be persuaded to part with at least some basic financial information prior to meeting a prospective investor. Likewise, American target investors usually understand that some time must be invested in personal interaction before "getting down to brass tacks." The education process is time-consuming but entirely necessary to the success of deals and my business. I am hopeful that as there is more and more interaction between the two cultures, the "gap" will narrow, especially as Chinese companies venture abroad and make foreign investments of their own.

Observations and Comments from Chinese Experts
Jiahai (John) Zhang
Panda Express, Area Coach Honolulu

Chinese traditionally look for cheap products and are focused on the short term because they couldn't afford things before; however, now the Chinese are changing and beginning to look for quality products at reasonable prices. At the same time, Chinese still bargain for prices, even if they are rich. You also see that Chinese like American-quality products more.

I believe that Americans are target- and context-focused. For example, if they visit distributors and end-users, it is because they are focused on those details. They have the attitude that they want to get to the target no matter what. They simply do not like to hear excuses. Once a target has been set, they also attack things with a can-do attitude. My suggestion here is for Hong Zhuang to find a different way to sell the locks. For example, he could focus on selling the locks to high-quality buildings or to other high-income buyers. These are precisely the people who will like American quality. They will look at it as the rich who need better protection for their assets.

On the other hand, I do not agree with Hong Zhuang's suggestion to lower the prices or to manufacture the locks in China. Chinese will prefer the American-brand locks. At the same time, I do agree that it might be helpful to create a new middle-range product that has the same brand name, as this will attract more end-users. It looks like Hong Zhuang needs to do more research and find out how much demand there is for the middle-range product. Then it becomes his job to persuade the company to accept his suggestions.

So, in my opinion, by understanding that Chinese culture is changing, ones sees that this will create new opportunities. This is especially the case in a change toward quality and pricing. Hong Zhuang should focus on this trend and sell high-quality locks at a higher price. He just needs to make sure to provide a great service and quality locks, and do so better than his competitors. With so many new buildings and with so many people who have more money, I am confident that there will be a big market for quality locks. It all depends on how you sell the locks.

CHANG QING (CHRIS) LI
INTERNATIONAL BUSINESS EXECUTIVE

As I read this scenario, I was reminded that the key to effective communication is to understand where both sides are coming from. Chinese communication style prefers hinting—providing all the background information but not raising the issue and not demanding things directly. We expect the other side to hear the meaning behind the words. Americans, however, like to cut to the chase. Personally, I have been in a lot of situations that are similar to Hong's in this case scenario. For example, we had an investment opportunity related to a new technology. Our general manager in China felt that it was very risky, and he was worried that there wasn't sufficient funding and doubted the continuing support of research and development. He presented all the data and left hints that this probably was not the time to invest; however, he never actually expressed his recommendation overtly. Even when the Americans asked him directly, he would continue to speak about the assumptions and conditions that would be necessary to make the investment successful. Just like what is mentioned in this case, he hoped that the Americans would understand his reservations from the context, but the Americans wanted a straight answer of yes or no. There is a deeper cultural background behind these communication styles that might help in understanding where the Chinese are coming from. The Chinese are afraid of losing face and taking responsibility when something goes wrong. So they are more risk averse, and they think more of a failed outcome. There is a Chinese proverb "枪打出头鸟 (qiāng dǎ chū tóu niǎo)," which means, "Shoot the bird that takes the lead." It warns people that you should not stick your neck out, otherwise you will be punished. This culture of fear is embedded in almost every Chinese, especially the older generation. We often ask ourselves, "Why should I be the one who makes the decision or takes the blame?" We think in terms of, "I provide the context, and you make the decision." On the other hand, American culture promotes individualism. It worships the hero. People are not afraid to speak out and express themselves. If Chinese and Americans do not know about this cultural difference, it can easily cause trust issues. I have heard many Americans complain to me that they can't get a straight answer when dealing with their Chinese counterparts. The Americans sometimes think that the Chinese are hiding something, but at the same time, the Chinese think that the Americans are forcing the issue or pretending that they don't understand something that is obvious. Fortunately, I do not believe that this problem is difficult to overcome. Communication can be drastically improved as long as this cultural difference is recognized and acknowledged between the two parties. In the case scenario, we see that the Americans were visiting the distributors and end-customers. My recommendation is they be patient during those visits, listen for the context, and take the time to understand where the Chinese are coming from and be aware of the challenges they, the Chinese, are facing. At the same time, I have noticed that Chinese are becoming more concise and more direct in their recommendations and decisions. As more business is being conducted between China and the United States, I have seen more people (both Chinese and American) making an effort toward the middle ground. I am not advocating changing your principles or bending the rules, but by purely acknowledging the existence of the cultural differences, we avoid many misunderstandings and potential loss of business opportunities.

WIE LI

SONY ERICSSON CHINA, CFO

The issues raised in this case are typical examples where the logical way of thinking between Western people and Chinese people is quite different. Western people have a direct way of thinking, and if they ask questions, they expect direct and honest answers, regardless of them being good or not. Chinese people tend to spread good news directly to the public; however, they choose to express bad news or their personal opinions in a more indirect way. For example, they may have a list of reasons to explain things before they reach the opinions or results.

In fact, talking in English in public is always a problem for Chinese people. When I was studying in the University of Adelaide in South Australia, I often noticed that most of the Chinese students would remain silent when lecturers asked them for questions or opinions; however, after the class, they would go up to the lecturer and ask their questions individually. This was probably from a lack of confidence in their English communication skills. The truth is Chinese tend to get nervous when they have to speak English in public; therefore, they avoid speaking in front of others, and they also worry about making mistakes and whether people can understand their English. Another thing I have noticed lately is when there is a problem that needs to be addressed, non-English speakers will get their local friends to talk to me on their behalf because they aren't always confident in their abilities to converse to me.

Of course, another problem is whenever these people are friends in a work group, or when they don't need to speak English, non-English speakers tend to talk in their first language. This is a missed opportunity because talking with their colleagues in English would be one of the best times for them to get to know and understand each other better. This will only help when they are involved in work-related issues later.

Trying to encourage staff to speak English, not only when they give reports to an overseas boss, but also in their daily working environment, is a positive to way to resolve these kinds of problems. At the same time, helping staff to build their confidence in using English is also essential. If the staff can get to know each other better and feel comfortable speaking English with native speakers, miscommunications can be reduced and eventually disappear.

Observations and Comments from the Authors

Wow, what excellent comments from the American and Chinese executives! Their examples, advice, and suggestions are spot on. As to communication styles, in this chapter we see many references to the tendency of North Americans to be more direct than the Chinese. Chang Qing Li was exactly right: Americans often feel that they cannot get a straight answer from the Chinese, and the Chinese are amazed that the Americans cannot take the hint. Why is this so? The references in this chapter to being context-focused or target-focused go back to what experts in intercultural communication refer to as "high-context" and "low-context" cultures—terms first used by the famous anthropologist Edward Hall. To be brief, in communication, we all have some information that is stored and some information that has to be overtly expressed. High-context cultures prefer to store more information. Low-context cultures prefer to overtly express information. To illustrate this, consider what happens to a couple that goes out on a first date. Since they do not know each other well, they have very little stored information. Consequently, they have to overtly say what their preferences are: chocolate ice cream, Italian food, romantic movies, country music, etc. On the other hand, a couple that has been married for thirty years has loads of stored information between the two of them. They can sit in the same room in comfortable silence, and when it is time to have a dessert, each already knows the preference of the other. If the wife asks, "Are you hot?" the husband knows that this really means, "Dear, I am hot, would you please turn on the air-conditioning."

Similar to couples on their first date, low-context individuals have less stored information, so they focus their communication on the actual words, both written and spoken. This is the tendency in North American culture. North Americans like to hear the actual words, write them down, follow specific guidelines, and know the rules. They want to hear, for example, "Yes, I do," "No, I don't," "Yes, we can," or "I will do it on Friday at 5:00 p.m." Behavior is dominated by the words that are overtly used. Chinese, on the other hand, are more like the couple that has been married for thirty years. They store information initially, and as a result, things are understood more than overtly stated.

In this case, we saw that Hong Zhuang was trying to explain to the Americans why the Chinese were sensitive to the cost of the locks, but none of his subtle hints were working. The Americans simply react better to specific data and hard facts. This is also the reason why the prospective American investors who Sandor Weiss talked about preferred detailed facts in fifty-page documents about the Chinese target companies. On the other hand, the Chinese company owners wanted to get to know their potential partners better before passing sensitive and confidential information on to them. The low-context Americans wanted the data; the high-context Chinese needed to store more information about their potential partners. The extra socializing and karaoke are not just time-fillers; for the Chinese, they are a chance to know their partners better. It is interesting to note that, in this case scenario, when the Americans made personal visits to the end-distributors, from the American perspective, they were gathering more information and data, but from the Chinese perspective, they were providing the extra context that the Chinese desired.

For those readers who want to discuss these issues further, consider the following topics and questions for discussion:

1. David Hollingsworth notes that while providing extra context is wonderful for a visit to the Forbidden City, it may actually get in the way of efficient work when one is focused mostly on results. In other words, the extra details get people lost in the main objective. How do you respond to this observation?

2. David Hollingsworth saw the Chinese desire to provide extra details as mere excuses and delays in getting to the root cause. The third participant helped bridge that miscommunication. In which scenarios is it better to teach the Chinese to be more direct, and in which scenarios is it better to teach the Americans to appreciate the extra details?

3. David Hollingsworth observes that the American management team has been successful for years in their business model, and Hong Zhuang should understand that. However, how does that correlate to the possibility that new strategies are needed in a new market?

4. What does it tell us when Sandor Weiss observes that often his role is to be a "cultural mediator," especially considering that his job is in the area of private equity investments?

5. Sandor Weiss is hopeful that as Chinese companies venture abroad more and make foreign investments, they will be more familiar with

the need to be more direct and transparent. What do you think of that?

6. It's interesting that Jiahai Zhang suggests that Hong Zhuang do more research to actually prove that there is a market and need for the middle-range product. In what ways would that actually help to make the decision and resolve this conflict?

7. Wie Li notes that Chinese have more difficulties in communicating bad news. Additionally, she has noticed that they will even send others to help communicate these ideas to her. What strategies can you give to work around this?

8. How do you respond to Chang Qing Li's example of the general manager in China who "hinted" at his reservations about the continued support of a project even though he never overtly expressed those doubts? Note that the Americans even asked the general manager directly and still didn't get a direct answer.

9. It seems that this dilemma is best resolved by meeting in the middle. How can one take advantage of the direct, focused communication of the West with the details, context, and observation of the East? In what ways would that help in this instance?

10. How does the "customer is always right" mindset relate to the issues in this scenario? Does it have anything to do with being direct or providing context?

3

CHINESE COOKBOOKS,
A LITTLE OF THIS AND THAT

Company: Shanghai VC

Focus: Opportunities in venture capital projects in Shanghai

Cultural Conflict: Americans' speech is precise, analytical, and quantifiable, each causing potential problems in communication with Chinese.

Introduction and Synopsis

In this scenario, Xin Qi provides a diverse list of items that might be summarized as things he would like to see evolve in China as Chinese professionals gain more and more international experience. These include things like how to be more precise in quantifying things, how to analyze situations more deeply, how to adjust performance expectations, what people mean by becoming more "modern," how to be more long-term focused, and how to manage human resources. As Ray Brimble mentions in his observations, Xin Qi's perception may be a bit fanciful, but it demonstrates the attitudes that many Chinese have. What is confirmed by all of the executive comments is Americans, indeed, focus a lot of attention on data and detailed analysis. Another pattern that emerges from this case is how difficult it is for Chinese to interact with their superiors. Coming from a culture where people strictly follow their bosses, it takes a while to get used to negotiating conditions, offering alternate opinions, or actually saying no. Jeff Cheng summarizes this by saying that Chinese come from a tradition of striving for a peaceful environment, while Americans search for rational and logical solutions. In reading this case, one gets the sense that, with time and maturity, the Chinese will also adapt to a new focus on sustainability as well.

Case Scenario

Xin Qi notes that if you want to understand the difference between Americans and Chinese, you should look at their cookbooks. Well, OK, that is not where one would expect to start when talking to a person who spent three years as the China business development manager for a telecommunications company and five years before that as a sales manager for a large computer company. Xin Qi's entrepreneurial spirit couldn't be confined to a single job or a specific cubicle, and he now finds himself working as a venture capitalist, centered mainly on projects in Shanghai. As to cookbooks, what Xin Qi notes is American cookbooks give you exact ingredients: two teaspoons of baking powder, one tablespoon of salt, etc. Chinese cookbooks generally tell you to add a little of this, a touch of that, and some of the other. Where Chinese cookbooks use adjectives to describe the foods, American cookbooks use quantifiers.

Similar to cookbooks, Xin Qi believes that American business practices are more precise and quantifiable. And he is also the first to tell you how much he admires that style. "Americans rule the business world. From MBA teaching theories to aggressive results-oriented deliverables, Americans have figured out how to do business." Xin Qi, by the way, completed his MBA at Stanford Graduate School of Business and then remained in the Bay Area for a few years working in Silicon Valley. "That start-up company was a great experience. I was amazed with how good the Americans were at getting at detailed specifics." Xin Qi recalled how when he first started, he'd say things like, "This market is big." His boss would then follow up by asking how big. He'd then get the details about how big, and his boss would still ask for more information, such as how he got his numbers or where the data came from. "My boss called this 'double-clicking.' He always knew how to get more and deeper information out of me." Before that experience, Xin Qi was, to use his words, "the typical Chinese who is used to the memorization of facts, but not used to their analysis." He adds, "Americans are better at analysis because they are used to asking more questions."

Not only does Xin Qi believe that Americans are adept at analyzing deep-level information, but he also thinks that it is part of their expectations. "Chinese need to adapt to the way that American companies put pressure on you to deliver and get results." During the three years he was with the telecommunications company, Xin Qi recalls that their revenues tripled, all the time retaining the same number of employees. The Chinese employees thought for sure that this meant that their salary should have increased by the same amount. It didn't, of course. What they didn't understand is this type of growth performance was expected. In fact, when revenues don't increase, people are put on notice.

For example, when Xin Qi worked for the computer company, they used a system where salespeople were reviewed every quarter. If someone wasn't able to produce standard levels for two consecutive quarters, they were put on notice for performance improvement. If things didn't improve by the third quarter, the employee was let go. "I remember one employee who was in charge of the southern region of China who had a hard time and couldn't reach our standard goals." Xin Qi adjusted assignments by putting the eastern region manager in charge of the south, hoping it would help the southern manager by having a new mentor. He knew it was a demotion of sorts, and unfortunately, over the next quarter, he still couldn't perform to standards. Of course, Xin Qi allowed him to resign before they had to let him go. All knew the pressure, and it was well understood that he would have to go. The point is Americans are used to this style because they are results-oriented. China is very pro-business, but there is not a tradition of firing people who do not excel at performance. "We have a tradition where the socialist market gave work to everyone without any concern for quality." According to Xin Qi, Chinese are learning to be more aggressive and results-oriented, and with that comes a greater focus on quality. At the same time, China also sees a growing sense of rich and poor as well as also a growing shift in labor laws to protect employees.

As part of this evolution, Xin Qi reminds us that the Chinese have defined modernization a little differently than most people in Western cultures. In the 1980s, as China was developing its economic reform and open policies, Deng Xiaoping used a well-known ancient term *xiǎokāng* to describe the objective of modernization in China. Translated, *xiǎokāng* means something like "small comfort" or "small well-being," referring to a situation where all citizens have advanced to the point where their basic needs in food and clothing have been met. Progress has been made, but there have also been criticisms of *xiǎokāng* because the rhetoric has always been limited to economic factors, while ignoring such social problems as moral standards and environmental issues. Consequently, Jintao Hu has presented a new aim of *dà tong*, or "harmonious society," to enhance the global needs of a modern society. Similarly, *dà tong* is an ancient term that refers more to the utopian ideal where everything is at peace. So, as Xin Qi sees it, the shift to where people emphasize quality fits well into the predominant goal of *dà tong*.

Interestingly enough, despite what Xin Qi says about being less precise, sometimes, especially with dealing with superiors, Chinese can also interpret words very literally. For example, Xin Qi remembers one time when his American manager told him that he expected $100 million in sales during the next quarter. The truth is the manager would have been happy with $80 million; he just said it to make him stretch. All Xin Qi heard, however, was the number $100 million. "Chinese will kill themselves to achieve $100 million because that is what they were told to do." Furthermore, Xin Qi notes that Chinese will kill themselves to achieve $100 million without asking for any help or more resources. Americans are more experienced at negotiating conditions with their bosses. They say things like, "OK, if you want $100 million, then I'm going to need Bob on my team." Xin Qi explains that it took him a long time to feel comfortable negotiating with his boss. "Sometimes, I knew what he was asking was impossible, but I found myself still wanting to say that I would do it." In China, people look at what their boss says with more of a military mindset. It is like getting orders from your superior, which you follow without question and without excuses. "Americans, on the other hand, expect to debate and negotiate options. We are still in that learning curve." However, he also adds that they are learning fast.

Xin Qi also thinks that Chinese professionals are in the learning curve to think with more of a long-term perspective. "I think Americans are better than we are at sustaining things over the long haul." Notwithstanding the dot-com and Wall Street syndrome, Xin Qi says Americans have more experience in maintaining things because of their ability to create added value. "Look at us, we build fake products!" cries Xin Qi. Furthermore, he believes that China's explosive growth—in Shanghai, for example—hasn't helped to get people out of a short-term focus, either. "I have a hard time getting people to think beyond three months. I wish they could think in terms of six or seven years." In fact, Xin Qi thinks that Chinese don't have to look only at Americans to see examples of how to maintain success and vision. "Look at Singapore," he says, thinking of their airport, "they planned it so well in advance. From their airport, you can get to anywhere in town in forty minutes. In Shanghai, we didn't even think far enough ahead to put the bathrooms on the same floor as where the flow of people is concentrated." Unlike the other areas that Xin Qi has mentioned, he believes that China is becoming even more focused on the short term instead of improving in their long-term focus.

One final area where Xin Qi sees differences between Americans and Chinese is in how they view the whole idea of human resources. "In fact, I'm not even sure if HR stands for 'human resources' or 'human relations.'" What he does know is, in the past, human resources was all about *guānxì*, where everything is directed at returning favors. Now, however, there is an increased sense that HR refers to resources: health and life insurance, stock options, and retirement benefits. In the past, HR referred to getting rewards, e.g., receiving metals and plaques, getting trips to Bali or Hawaii, having your picture taken with the boss with all of your family present to see the event. "Here in China, we have a long way to go to learn how to manage human resources instead of human relations, but we're learning."

So it is a long list of areas where Xin Qi senses a need for increased development. But, as he said in the beginning when referring to Chinese cookbooks, "We are working on a little of this and a little of that. Just wait and see how it all turns out."

Observations and Comments from American Experts
RAYMOND J. BRIMBLE
LYNXS GROUP, PRESIDENT AND CEO

Like the other vignette writers, Xin Qi's observations reflect his own personal style, and in this case, it is the worldview of a Silicon Valley

MBA. Xin Qi equates that world with "American business" in general. He attributes certain universal values to American business, which, while very generous, may give the typical American businessperson way too much credit. In his fantasy world, most Americans ask all the right questions, do perfect analysis including multiple drill-downs to get the salient facts, expect and get 100 percent per year sales growth every year, and always have long-term perspectives on all business decisions. American readers are no doubt chuckling at this already! The truth is we stumble around, make educated guesses, fail to meet our sales goals, think no further than the next quarter, and are dead wrong in our assumptions much of the time. Often, the only difference is we have better rhetoric and more established business theories. We know how to use graphs and PowerPoint presentations so that it appears to others that we always have the answers. Chinese readers should not assume that, as Americans, we always know what we are talking about, no matter how well we talk the talk.

But what we do best is adapt. Xin Qi mentions that Chinese employees are more used to approaching tasks with a "military mind," whereas Americans approach business plans in a less literal way. Quite right. But he does not see his own contradiction in describing American analysis and planning, along with the equal ability to be flexible. To use military jargon again, the famous German Field Marshall Helmuth von Moltke once said, "No battle plan survives contact with the enemy." This was to say, no matter how hard you plan, when the battle starts, you have to adapt. Interestingly enough, Xin Qi recognizes this same phenomenon, not on the battlefield, but in the Chinese kitchen. Chinese cooks have a recipe, but no need to get too hung up on every little detail. Believe it or not, most American cooks end up preparing their masterpieces "with a little pinch of this and a little pinch of that," too.

From my experience, I like the way that Chinese businesses can launch things. They know how to create something from nothing. As things mature, in Shanghai, and throughout China, I imagine that Chinese businesses will learn to focus more on sustainability than just "launch, make as much money as quickly as you can, and then prepare for the worst." The inevitable downturn will teach this lesson, and the survivors will have a more sustainable long-term view. But, for now, keep looking at the cookbook, but don't be afraid to think up a few recipes while you're at it.

Karen Boyer
Goodwill Industries of Central Texas, Special Events Coordinator

Xin Qi's observation about the differences between Chinese and American cookbooks is spot on. Taking cooking lessons in China at several popular restaurants lead me to the same conclusion. When I first arrived in China, I fell in love with all of the delicious foods that were so different from the ones I had tried in American Chinese restaurants. I wanted to be able to share these delectable dishes with my family when I returned to the States, so I negotiated cooking classes in exchange for American culture and language lessons at several local restaurants. The food I made with the cooks' help was always wonderful. However, each time I returned to my apartment to recreate these dishes, what I ended up with was inedible—I guess it's take out again! Although I had asked for measurements to help me cook better, they didn't quite understand what it was that I needed, given that they had never used them.

This problem was solvable with better communication. If I had demanded that they give me more exact measurements, it would have done me no good. Instead, sharing information about my culture and showing my interest in theirs was what was needed to reach a solution. I brought in some of my favorite Thanksgiving Day recipes and showed them how to cook some classical American holiday foods. I was able to explain how our recipes were written and also let them know why I was having trouble recreating their dishes. Although they thought the American style of cooking was very humorous, they understood my difficulty and did their best to write down some recipes, which I still have today. Chinese people, like Americans, are very proud of their culture. Showing a genuine interest in their culture will not only open lines of communication, but also gives you the information needed to be successful.

Once, when I was teaching a class of college students, I gave them an assignment to bring in some pictures of their childhood. The students all wrote the assignment down and promised to bring in their pictures. When I got to class the next week, only a few students brought in their pictures. I was surprised because the students had always turned in their assignments on time. I found out the students had agreed to the assignment out of politeness, even when knowing that they could not complete it, as their pictures were in their hometowns, which were far from the city where the school was located. If I had started by asking them if they had any pictures and where they were, I would have soon found that this assignment was best left for after the New Year, when they would all have had a chance to go home and bring back some pictures, which they did, and we were able to successfully complete the lesson. I found the best approach was to ensure that the students had the tools necessary to complete the project successfully before assigning it.

The same principles of communication through general cultural interest also apply to the business world. The best way to know that your meaning is understood is to probe deeper with follow-up questions. Both giving and getting examples is also very beneficial. By delving deeper into the Chinese culture as you explain the Western culture, you will be setting a respectful and positive tone to your meetings.

JEFF BOCK
MICROCONTROLLER SOLUTIONS GROUP, GLOBAL MARKETING MANAGER

I refer to a number of the issues that Xin Qi discusses as the "*Lǎobǎn* Syndrome." *Lǎobǎn* is the Mandarin word for "boss," but it has a much more rigid meaning in Chinese culture than it does in American culture. American people are trained to respect their bosses and work hard for them, but in my personal experience, a two-way communication path between boss and employee is not only encouraged, but it is absolutely critical. In China, most employees are accustomed to one-way communication from boss to employee, and open dialogue with your boss is not a portion of your relationship with your manager.

The *Lǎobǎn* Syndrome became particularly clear to me after six months of living and working in Shanghai. I'm responsible for leading a global team but have recently been particularly focused on building, training, and developing a team to focus on our Asia-Pacific region based in Shanghai. During the start-up phase of hiring this team, I did not expect much challenge from employees, but one day, I realized that I had been there over six months, and nobody on my team had ever disagreed with me! I usually have over twenty people disagreeing with me over e-mail from America and Europe even before I turn on my computer in the morning! Xin Qi indicates that people would not disagree with him even if they knew what he was asking for was not possible—and his employees would just say yes in order to avoid conflict. I have seen this often, so I've had to become a bit better at spotting the *Lǎobǎn* syndrome, as outlined below:

- A typical Chinese employee is not willing to disagree with their *Lǎobǎn*, either in public or in private, so in order to pull out their opinions and create open dialogue, it is absolutely necessary to build a trusting relationship with them and paint them a very clear picture of success—success that involves all aspects of the project, including hitting milestones, achieving quality, reaching business goals, and doing all of this without dragging dead bodies across the finish line.

- If members of your team agree with a challenge you give to them, ask them why they think they can complete it, how are they going to do it, what challenges they think they will face, and what they will do to overcome those issues. If they cannot articulate the reasoning, then I find it best to perhaps help them understand the context and offer suggestions for how to handle it.

- Celebrate when people avoid pitfalls, and continue to them coach if they unfortunately make an error. It is just as important to publicly acknowledge not only that someone did a good job on a project, but also have them discuss with the rest of the team *how* they made it successful. Describing it on their own will make a powerful lesson for the rest of your Chinese team.

It is critically important to overcome the *Lǎobǎn* Syndrome if you hope to achieve optimal results—that is, unless you are able to always have the best idea in the room, and you are able to do all of the work yourself! I didn't think you could....

Observations and Comments from Chinese Experts
SHOU ZHENG (JEFFREY) CHENG
RUSSELL REYNOLDS ASSOCIATES, OPERATIONS MANAGER

Chinese and Americans get along well in most companies in the United States. But it is true, compared to most Americans, Chinese are relatively quiet and "less opinionated" on many topics that need brainstorming at meetings. There are two main reasons behind it. First is language. English is still the second language to many Chinese, unless you are American-born Chinese. It's not easy for them to defend their own opinions in a second language with many Americans. Furthermore, when Chinese use their second language to respond to questions, it usually causes what I call a "half-step" delayed response. This would be totally different if they were using their own language—Mandarin. Second, there is a difference in philosophy. Eastern philosophy is based on the principle that "the fundamentals of the status quo should not be questioned." People from many Eastern countries avoid direct confrontation with each other. They understand that "face" is important to most people. They don't like to be challenged or to challenge others. Basically, they prefer to comprise in order to return to a "peaceful environment." Western philosophy focuses more on rational and logical solutions to all questions. So Western employees prefer to raise all questions before they execute the task. In most cases, American employees think Chinese employees are indifferent to discussion or less responsive, and they feel frustrated by a "less productive" meeting with Chinese colleagues.

As to my own experience, I joined a firm where I am the only Chinese employee in the Houston office. Initially, I was a little quiet at staff meetings, even when I thought of some good, but different ideas. My thinking was that I was the "freshman," and I didn't want to confront my colleagues, even when I thought that I was right. Initially, I preferred to have one-on-one and face-to-face meetings with my colleagues in a small office. Gradually, however, I realized that it is not right when you have good ideas but don't share them with others, even if it may cause some fights among you and colleagues. So I started to say more things at the staff meetings, and it became easier to raise different opinions and questions about the potential issues that might come up in my projects. It is now a year later, and I think I have won the respect from my colleagues, and I have also made some good friends from different "fights" among us.

As to my suggestions, if you are a Chinese who works in an American company, please speak directly and act directly. It may be difficult at the beginning, but you will get used to it. If you do not feel confident in your English compared to the "mother tongue" of your American colleagues, the best thing to do is open your mouth widely and speak slowly and clearly. Everyone knows that English is your second language, so you don't need to be afraid of your Chinese accent or your slow speaking speed. Show your confidence with smart and well-prepared answers.

JULIA WU
DELL COMPUTER, SENIOR MANAGER IN WORLDWIDE PROCUREMENT

Well, it is very interesting to start talking about American and Chinese culture by comparing cookbooks. Since I never cook, I went to the bookstore and checked out a cookbook; XinQi is not exactly right. The Chinese cookbook states the following ingredients: three hundred grams of chicken meat, one-third teaspoon of salt, one tablespoon of soy sauce, etc. Oh well, maybe XinQi hasn't looked at cookbooks for a while.

I fully agree about American business being quantified. Nobody in my organization will ever forget the severe shortage that happened during quarter three of last year when we had hundreds, even thousands, of customer orders in hand, but we couldn't deliver the products due to a parts shortage. At that time, management would ask us what the day's backlog was, how many we could fill, or what the products' "short to backlog" data was. They wanted to know which parts were being built and how soon we would be able to pull in the material. The whole management team up to Michael was reviewing the shortage status of the data daily, and everyone worked to mitigate the impact on the customers' experience. Given the high exposure of what we were doing, the Chinese employees were very much motivated. This never would have happened if it had been a Chinese company.

The second thing that I would like to mention is job security. In my parent's generation, Chinese people didn't have to worry about losing their job. Once the government assigned a person to a job, he or she would be working in that position for thirty to forty years until retirement. It didn't matter if he or she did well or poorly, he or she would never worry about losing a job. Unless a person was found guilty of criminal acts, nobody would ever be fired. For young professionals today, we have started to learn and adapt to what was called *dà guō fàn*, which no longer applies. There is no more social communist job security. The only way to secure a job nowadays is to improve capabilities, increase market value, and competitive marketing. It doesn't surprise me at all that someone in sales would be told that if they didn't reach their sales quota for three months that they would fired, especially if an improvement plan had been put in their place. Traditionally, Chinese people would not expect to be fired for not delivering results, but gradually, it is becoming more and more acceptable. A popular strategy I have seen among my peers who are Chinese managers is to find a way to reassign an employee to a new position that isn't as easily quantified. For example, they will put a low performer into a less important position where there is no pay increase and fewer opportunities. As a result, the employee ends up resigning, and this is the best way for both sides to avoid "losing face." I personally don't agree with this because I think that holding on to a low-performer is a waste of time and company resources. A manager should have the courage to fire an underperforming employee.

The third area that I would like to highlight is that of hierarchy. Not only in China, but also in all of Eastern Asia, including Japan, South Korea, Singapore, etc., all corporations are hierarchy-based companies. We are educated to respect the teacher and the supervisor. Traditionally, we don't challenge a superior's decision; instead, we strictly follow it. When I first joined Dell, I was coached by my mentor, and the first thing we learn in an American company is how to say no. This is a tough conflict from a Chinese mindset. It works pretty well in a multinational, especially American, companies. In other situations and industries, however, the American way doesn't work as well. For example, right now I'm managing several PC manufactories, some of which are Asian and some American. It is clear that the Asian companies have more discipline, quicker decision-making capabilities, and better execution than the American companies. This is because Asian companies rarely experience any pushback.

JULIA GUO HUIMIN
CHINDEX MEDICAL LTD., OPERATION DIRECTOR

I agree with Xin Qi's conceptual view; Americans are better at making quantitative statements and in analyzing problems, based on which they make expectations and follow up with results. But the Chinese are more conceptual and artistic when they think and talk about problems. They try to achieve an "almost" or "about the same" status. The characteristics of Chinese people are related to our cultural and educational system.

Historically, the study of liberal arts has been emphasized, the purpose of which is to become an official rather than being able to do certain things. Only engineers have traditionally had to quantify problems, while being an official meant a focus on philosophy—and the more vague, the better. It has only been in modern times that we have begun to focus on science and technology, but the history of this is short, and the traditional philosophy of society becoming an official rather than doing things has not been completely transferred over. Therefore, in Chinese culture, there is more flexibility in seeing things both ways. For example, it is very difficult to translate a Chinese official's speech. It is not the competence of the translator, but it's the conceptual things that the officials say, such as *dà tong* ("harmony"), what *dà tong* is (what harmony is), and what we need to achieve in the next five years that can be considered *dà tong* (harmony). Politicians simply will not say that clearly, which is also the same with American politicians.

I have been working with Americans, and I share Xin Qi's opinion. Bosses from Western cultures will ask you how much bigger the market is expected to be this year and where you get your data from, and they expect you to use other related data to support your expectations and explanations. However, the Chinese colleagues only draw a blueprint, and they happily talk about it, but they are not asked details about it. Or they also go to the other extreme and don't make any effort to understand or even look at the data, and sometimes, they even make data up. On one hand, this is because the Chinese people are not used to analyzing what they are doing; they have no idea what the boss will ask about first, and they don't know how to prepare for it. On the other hand, because the analysis and data are not emphasized, management decisions are made without them. Interestingly, my personal experience can illustrate the complexity and unreliability of predicting things in China. My job is periodically predicting the monthly, quarterly, and annual sales; enforcing contracts; distributing goods; and getting the customer's certificate of receipt before the monthly or annual reports are to arrive, all to include them in the current sales revenues. Based on the American way of doing things, these are all predictable and easily obtained. That is to say, for example, the main factors are when the contract is signed, the production cycle, the delivery date, etc. All of these factors have a controllable and predictable lead-time. In China, however, basically all of these items have uncontrollable factors. It may be that clients delay purchasing because of personnel changes, delivery cycles, or delays in provinces other than around Beijing and Shanghai; delivery times may vary more than twenty days in remote areas because airplanes cannot get to certain places, only trucks can transport them, or the road might be blocked because of weather conditions. These are all unpredictable factors.

This case mentions that China used to be a socialist country and that the people are not results-oriented. In my opinion, that was twenty or thirty years ago. Chinese people are more results-oriented than ever now, but they sometimes do not pay attention to the feasibility of the process or their methods. So if the management of an international company sets a goal or gives a task to a Chinese team, they will do their best to complete it, without any bargaining and without asking for reasonable resources, all because in Chinese culture "listen and follow" is one of the most important ways to show respect. Management in international companies should not only focus on "results," but they also need to make sure that the process is reasonable and legal.

If I were to offer a suggestion from my experience, I would recommend that Americans who focus on understanding and analyzing data realize that the data in China is not always reliable. On the other hand, Chinese people understand the importance of being results-oriented. The pressure of competition encourages everyone to struggle to meet expectations—if they agree with your expectations. You just have to follow through by understanding his difficulties and the support he needs. If so, good outcomes will come. Chinese are not good at collaboration by asking for resources, they prefer individual heroism. The boss needs to take the initiative to understand what is needed so that all can finish the task better. For the Chinese employees, if you want to work in an American company, you have to know the rules of the game before you play. To negotiate, you will need to use data, analysis, and quantitative proof, all so that you can get the resources you need as well as to eliminate unrealistic expectations.

Observations and Comments from the Authors

Social scientists sometimes subdivide cultural tendencies among those who are universalists and those who are particularists. The universalists are those who try to standardize everything and apply the same rules to all situations. On the other hand, the particularists are the ones who see the unique and different in everything. North Americans are traditionally thought of as having strong tendencies toward universalism. The analysis of data, the efforts to get more and more detailed information, the focus on being results-oriented, and the emphasis on quality are all by-products of universalist cultures. Of course, there are advantages to both types of approaches, and today's world of international business is a good example of the blending of the two. On one side, business can be more efficient when people base decisions on reliable and detailed data. On the other side, creativity often implies the flexibility to think in new ways.

In this case, Xin Qi finds himself in the middle of both of these worlds, especially as it relates to how he works with his superiors. Xin Qi even mentions that Chinese will kill themselves to achieve a stated objective, even when deep down they know that the boss never stated the objective in absolute terms (or even if stated in absolute terms, never intended them to be interpreted that way). Note that Jeff Cheng mentioned a similar observation in his comments when he said that he had to learn to express and defend his feelings in front of others. Initially, his tendency was to keep his opinions to himself or to later discuss them with people in private. With time, however, he realized that it was important for him to share those opinions in public. It was quite a transition for him. Julia Wu similarly added that the first thing she had to learn when working in an American company was to say no. At the same time, Julio Guo Huimin offered the caution that there are a number of factors that are uncontrollable in China. As such, the data is not always reliable.

It is important for universalists to remember that one of the reasons why they can depend on data is because there is confidence in the accuracy of the numbers. Particularist societies traditionally do not have that luxury. Instead, they always have to creatively modify things to fit the current situation because there is no reliable measurement standard. For example, in universalist cultures, when there is a car accident, people immediately call the police to make a report of the event. This is because there is a confidence that laws will apply in universal and predictable ways. When there are accidents in particularist cultures, there is often an attempt to resolve things individually before the police arrive. That is to say, since there is no guarantee that everyone will follow the standard laws, it ends up being better to resolve things on an individual basis. Xin Qi's comments show that Chinese are still working within both systems.

The following is a number of questions based on the executive's comments. For those who wish to discuss this topic more, these questions provide possibilities for starting points:

1. Ray Brimble observes that Xin Qi may be giving the Americans too much credit for perfect analysis and organization. How much of this is really related to knowing what to do versus making educated guesses?

2. Discuss the nature of innovation and launching things as compared to sustainability. How does this apply to business practices in China?

3. Speaking of Xin Qi's contradiction in describing the American's analysis and planning, while also being impressed with their flexibility and ability to adapt, is there any reason why this balance would be different between U.S. and Chinese cultures?

4. What do you think about Jeff Bock's idea about the *Lǎobǎn* Syndrome? Does the two-way versus one-way communication describe a significant difference between American and Chinese style?

5. Jeff Bock provides three suggestions to combat the *Lǎobǎn* Syndrome: Paint a clear picture of success; have them articulate why, how, and what they are doing to reach their goals; and acknowledge successes and what made them successful. Is it possible to implement these suggestions without being condescending, or is that even an issue?

6. If part of the reason that Chinese are reticent to offer opinions is because of limitations to their English-language skills, what suggestions do you have to address this issue?

7. Julia Wu observes that, a generation ago, people didn't worry about losing their jobs. What was lost and what was gained by having a new generation that no longer applies *dà guō fàn*?

8. Although Julia Wu was coached by her mentor to learn how to say no, she also observes that this doesn't apply as well in all situations, especially when working with Asian manufactories. How does one strike the balance?

9. This case mentions a transition from a socialist market where everyone had work to a more aggressive and results-oriented market where the

focus is on quality and production. What aspects of the old system would be most beneficial to be retained?

10. Why is it that a culture (and language) that leave so much unsaid and inferred from the context end up interpreting the actual English words so literally?

11. Describe your understanding of the difference between human resources and *Guānxì*?

4

WHAT A COOL LICENSE PLATE

Company: Worldwide Energy Providers (WEP)
Focus: Generation and distribution of electricity worldwide
Cultural Conflict: Americans expect a direct solution to problems, based on the presentation of evidence and facts. This may not coincide with Chinese style.

Introduction and Synopsis

In this case, we note how much Ning Yang appreciates the Americans' tendency to directly confront issues and seek an immediate solution. He provides a number of examples of how Chinese professionals do not have the tradition of attacking problems head-on. First, he talks about an instance where the Chinese workers had evidence to defend their opinion, but they preferred to e-mail it to everyone after the meeting instead of orally presenting the information during the meeting. Then he shares some stories in regard to working with subcontractors that also illustrate the need for personal attention and follow up—so much so that the shop manager even ended up sleeping at the factory! Nearly all of the executives, both the North Americans as well as the Chinese, comment on this case by bringing up the topic of face. Arnold Pachtman goes so far as to say that the title of the case could have been "Zen and the Art of Giving Face and Building Relationships." He even wonders why North Americans somehow got left without a "face gene." All of the executive comments point to the same recommendation: Do not minimize the importance of giving others prestige and status, building personal relationships, and working hard at preserving face. At the end of this case, Jeff Poulter receives a gift—a Chinese license plate to add to his collection. From an America perspective, this is simply a nice gift, but from a Chinese perspective, this is an excellent example of evidence that a successful personal relationship has been established.

Case Scenario

Ning Yang is the first to say that he admires how when Americans find a problem, they attack it to find a solution. With a vision for the future, he observes, "We don't always do that here in China. When there is a problem in China, people often try to avoid it or make concessions and compromises." Currently, Ning Yang is the business development manager of North China for Worldwide Energy Providers (WEP), an electric company that specializes in the distribution of electricity around the world. Ning Yang has been with WEP for the past five years, having previously worked as a project director for a company that specializes in solar power and wave technologies. WEP is one of the world's leading power companies, with nearly 150 power plants across the globe, generating electricity to nearly 150 million people. Their 35,000 employees are spread throughout nearly 30 different countries, including China, where they have been since the early 1990s.

So what was Ning Yang referring to with this comment about how Americans attack problems head-on? He easily provides some examples. A week prior, there was a meeting to discuss employee benefits and employment. The Chinese HR manager conducted the meeting with a number of U.S. colleagues who were also present. Every issue that was brought up was followed up by comments from the Americans, who brought their own perspective to the situation. The Chinese were basically, well, silent. "They just weren't participating as much in the discussion." During a break in the meeting, however, Ning Yang noticed how much more the issues were being discussed among the Chinese attendees. As it turns out, the company was having a hard time bringing talent into a second-tier city. There had been a low acceptance rate after an offer was made. It was becoming a huge problem because they couldn't hire anyone. Basically, the Americans felt that it was a supply issue because there were no good candidates. They presented this opinion fairly forcefully, you might say even aggressively. On the other hand, the Chinese thought that the issue was more related to low pay and the undesirability associated with living in second-tier cities. As they saw things, there were plenty of good candidates, they just weren't willing to live away from the first-rate action of places like Shanghai. Although this is how the Chinese employees saw things, it isn't anything they actually said during the meeting. During the meeting, they didn't offer any evidence for their argument, and they didn't answer any of the questions that the Americans brought up in the meeting. They simply said that they would look into things. Bottom line, they weren't comfortable confronting the Americans directly during the meeting. Sociologists who deal with cultural issues claim that, in some countries, subordinates have historically had little influence on the decisions that are made by their superiors. In these cultures, there would be no reason to openly offer suggestions to your superior. Traditionally, China has been classified in those terms. Interestingly enough, however, after the meeting, the Chinese did send e-mails to everyone with the data and information, which showed that, indeed, there was a healthy pool of candidates to draw from. It was the exact information and evidence that was needed to defend their position. They simply felt uncomfortable presenting it at the meeting, preferring to send it as an e-mail later on.

This isn't to say that Chinese do not like personal, face-to-face contact. The truth is they do. They just want to avoid direct confrontations in meetings. In fact, Ning Yang recalls a similar experience from a few years ago when he was trying to secure visas for some American expats. The government officials wanted to talk to the Americans face to face. The Americans, however, didn't want to waste their time because, as they saw it, "all the information that they needed was already on the form that they filled out." They just couldn't see why it would be important to go in person. So the government officials got upset, basically saying that the Americans weren't showing them any respect. And, naturally, all of this resulted in a delay in getting the approvals for the expat's visas. Finally, Ning Yang convinced the Americans that they should go in to see the officials. In the end, the face-to-face visits were positive and all worked out by approving the visas. "You see," summarizes Ning Yang, "face-to-face meetings are important, but so is avoiding confrontation."

WEP also works a lot with subcontractors who do much of the local manufacturing. Ning Yang notes that he often sees this less-than-direct attack of problems in the way that local shop managers conduct business. Recently, for example, there was a quality-control issue with one of their subcontracted manufacturers in Jiangsu Province, just outside of Nanjing. It wasn't easy to resolve because the shop supervisor kept minimizing the importance of the problem. An American engineer, Jeff Poulter, who was working with Ning Yang, had identified the exact problem, so the two of them talked directly to the shop manager about it. However, it soon became evident that it wasn't enough to make him aware of the quality problem. The shop supervisor just didn't relate to the importance of the problem. He made excuses and seemed to shrug it off. Jeff was becoming frustrated because the facts were plainly laid out, and there was no rational reason to deny what was going on. Finally, Ning Yang suggested that it might be more beneficial to discuss these matters with the shop supervisor in a different setting, away from the shop itself. So a series of dinners (a number of times) followed where it became easier to discuss things while mixing business with less formality. These dinners seemed to change things to the point where the shop supervisor was so motivated to improve the quality performance of his shop that he began to sleep at the factory! He wanted to be there all the time, following up on things and keeping track of 100 percent of the operations. Jeff was amazed. Before the dinners, he had been preparing for the possibility of closing the subcontracting relationship. Now, just a few weeks later, the shop manager was sleeping at the factory. "It's not enough to make people aware of the regulations, you have to become friends, too," added Ning Yang. "You can't expect the subcontracting company to work on autopilot. They need your constant attention." Ning Yang knows that this implies frequent visits to the factory, verifying that things are going as previously agreed upon.

Ning Yang had a similar experience with another subcontractor in Hefei who had been hired to build some component parts. When the American team first discussed things with this company, they stressed the importance of delivering the products on time. There was a steep penalty in the United States for late work. Whenever the component parts were late, it slowed up the process for everyone, implying a heavy financial penalty. It turns out that the Chinese company didn't really understand all of the details. In fact, Ning Yang found out later that the subcontractor company's lawyer, who they had used to write up the contract, was really a criminal lawyer. He didn't understand much of the business side of things. And among the things that he didn't understand was sending products CFR. The company thought that once the product was built that was the end of their obligation. In this case, the product was extremely large and could only be shipped on special cargo ships, which don't leave from port every day. This requires special planning and organization. Since the suppliers in Hefei didn't understand the Incoterms (international commercial terms), they thought their job was done. As a result, WEP ended up losing a lot of time, and they incurred numerous fines. When the parts finally did arrive in the United States, WEP had to pay its workers overtime to try to catch up on the work. So, in this instance, not only did the subcontractor company not understand the global implications of late work, they also didn't follow the written documents, because they didn't fully understand them.

Despite these examples, Ning Yang is also quick to observe that things are much better now than they were a few years ago. There is a younger generation of management teams that understand these issues better. "We also see a number of companies who are trying to get international standard certificates." Ning Yang notes that, in the past, people were really good at completing paperwork, but not as efficient at actually doing what is on paper. The new push for certification has changed things. Because of this, Ning Yang also notes how much Chinese appreciate the training that Americans give them. "It is one of the Americans' strengths."

Almost as an aside, there is an interesting ending to this story. The engineer Jeff Poulter recently spent some time training a crew from Shanghai. He has learned how to connect with his Chinese colleagues, and they enjoyed the training so much that they wanted to give him a gift. One of Jeff's hobbies is to collect license plates, including ones from all over the world. In China, people need to turn in their expired license plates. So it is very difficult to find old ones. In this instance, however, the Chinese partners found some plates for him, and he was delighted. He also understood how big of a deal it was for them to find the plates, both in the effort it took to get them and in what it meant for their working relationship. It looks like Jeff has come a long way from when he first approached the shop supervisor with his rationally presented facts.

Observations and Comments from American Experts

ARNOLD PACHTMAN (BAI WENAN)

L-3 COMMUNICATIONS GLOBAL SECURITY & ENGINEERING SOLUTIONS

This case could be aptly titled "Zen and the Art of Giving Face and Building Relationships." "Face" (prestige or esteem) is a concept that is central to relationships in nearly every country in the world. Yet, due to a historical and cultural fluke, North Americans seem to lack the "face gene" and fail to understand its importance overseas. Face has deep roots in China; feudalism, Confucianism, communism, nationalism, and human nature all reinforce the concepts of looking good before peers and superiors, deferring to those with authority, and avoiding open conflict. Face can be more important to Chinese than the substance of a relationship. Giving face to Chinese colleagues raises their esteem in the eyes of superiors and gives face to their organizations as well.

Another concept that Chinese view quite differently than North Americans is relationships. Chinese view all relationships as arising out of *yuán fèn* ("destiny"). Unlike in North America, where we draw a clear line between business and personal affairs, Chinese relationships reside with individuals, not positions, titles, or companies. By building a personal relationship, Chinese and North American colleagues will also strengthen their working relationship.

But what does all of this have to do with confronting problems head-on? Here are some important face-giving and relationship-building lessons from the case:

- *"When there is a problem in China, people often try to…make concessions and compromises."* Open conflict is costly and destructive to face and relationships.
- *"[The Americans] presented this opinion fairly forcefully, you may even say aggressively."* This public, direct challenge by a guest was rude and made the Chinese hosts lose face.
- *"[The Chinese] weren't comfortable confronting the Americans directly during the meeting."* To the Chinese hosts, a direct counter would

have caused an even bigger loss of face to both sides and would have damaged the developing relationship.

- *"The government officials wanted to talk to the Americans face to face... The Americans weren't showing them any respect."* Chinese officials would have gained face from the meeting, and a direct relationship could have benefitted both sides. The Americans' refusal to meet with Chinese officials was the height of arrogance.

- *"Face-to-face meetings are important, but so is avoiding confrontation."* Face-to-face meetings give face and build relationships, but confrontation destroys both.

- *"It might be more beneficial to discuss these matters with the shop supervisor...away from the shop itself."* The shop supervisor would have lost huge face if he was rebuked and forced to acknowledge a quality problem in front of his subordinates.

- *"[At] a series of dinners...it became easier to discuss things while mixing business with less formality."* The dinner invitations gave the supervisor huge face and established a direct relationship with the American engineer.

- *"It's not enough to make people aware of the regulations, you have to become friends."* In China, there are regulations for everything, but *relationships* make things happen.

- *"[The American] understood how big of a deal it was for them to find the plates, both in the effort it took to get them and in what it meant for their working relationship."* This exchange of goodwill gave face to both sides and strengthened the relationship.

As to my suggestions, there are easy ways to give face and build relationships:

- *Family:* An excellent way to strengthen relationships is to meet your Chinese colleagues on a day off and avoid discussing business. Sharing family photographs and stories about your family and community life presents a side of you that Chinese strongly relate to and appeals to the intense curiosity Chinese have about foreign guests.

- *Contacts:* Offering to help your Chinese colleagues network with your business or personal contacts back home will add the weight of potential future relationships to your relationship with them. Once established, relationships are valuable, enduring collateral that follows individuals, not companies.

- *Gifts*: Token gifts and small favors give face and show esteem or gratitude; however, gifts are also a favorite way to create obligations. Depending on how a gift is given and received, it can become either an advantage or a burden. Gifts are usually safe if they are small, symbolic, and presented in the context of the relationship[1].

- *Helping*: To the Chinese, the simple phrase "I will help you (task)" is a powerful statement of caring, and a commitment to the relationship. Do not sound condescending, and make sure your Chinese colleagues understand that you are making the offer out of friendship, and a genuine desire to make them happy. Then do it! Your colleagues will inevitably be delighted and reciprocate with enthusiasm.

By understanding and practicing the art of face-giving and relationship-building in China, North Americans will be able to work harmoniously with their Chinese colleagues and resolve the most difficult issues together.

MAGNUS & MINGXING LARSEN
MANDMX.COM, FOUNDERS AND CREATORS

I have always known that Americans were more direct than Chinese in most situations, but now I have a specific example and situation to illustrate that idea. These are such fascinating situations that the reader will need to continuously read this book so as to remember the solutions.

First, Ning Yang observed that, in the meeting about second-tier city candidates, the Chinese didn't speak up about their correct observations of the situation, even when the Americans forcefully presented their incorrect ideas. While working in Shanghai for a number of years, I could see that my Chinese colleagues were not comfortable in speaking or participating at the weekly meetings, and whenever there was a break or the end of the meeting, they constantly chatted away about the issues raised in the meeting. At the same time, I could see, as an American, I had more confidence in the meeting to raise questions and point out issues, and even disagree with other colleagues. But knowing a bit more about the Chinese culture and attitude,

---

[1] *Negotiating with the Chinese: Getting to "Hao!"* by A. Pachtman, Corporate Counsel's International Advisor, No. 169, p. 11, June 1, 1999

I know that the American method would very rarely happen with the local workers. Participation would be totally normal and actually welcomed from the Chinese colleagues since they were there and part of the group, but that would rarely happen. I could only imagine if the HR manager who conducted the meeting was an American and how exasperating that would be when he got the e-mail from the Chinese colleagues after the meeting! "We were in a meeting, and you had every opportunity to present those facts and you chose not to! *Why?*" I wonder if the Chinese HR manager who actually conducted the meeting was ready for the forceful response from the Americans and if it made him uncomfortable.

I think it is very humorous that the Americans in this scenario had an idea, presented it forcefully, and that was that. No more discussion. In fact, the correct answer was the complete opposite. Mingxing told me that she immediately had the feeling that, with the second-tier city, the company would have to pay me more money to make me live away from Shanghai. That would make it more attractive. She noted that Shanghai people would go through culture shock even moving to a second-tier city a province away.

In the end, whoever is conducting a meeting like this needs to make it clear that everyone speaks so as not to naturally gravitate to those who enjoy speaking. If everyone participates and only the one conducting the meeting has the final say, then no one participant will have the final say. The other solution that actually presented itself in the description is taking a break in the middle of the meeting. This would be very wise, not to just use the facilities, but to hear the chatter of the people as they are free to chat about what they want. If you heard what the Americans were talking about during the break, it was probably about Red Sox baseball or Texas football, not about second-tier cities and qualified candidates. But the Chinese were talking about those things, and Ning Yang is culturally aware of this. While overhearing these things, he should purposefully go over to them and tell them that they must present those ideas when the break is over. When the meeting reconvenes, he can call out the Chinese colleagues, and then they will present their ideas.

Secondly, the story of Jeff Poulter and the guy who slept at the factory is a fascinating one. It illustrates not so much that Americans can pinpoint the problem and attack it, but it more forcefully illustrates the cultural finesse that businesspeople need to employ with some of the people in China. What Jeff and Ning Yang had to demonstrate to the factory supervisor was that they cared for him and they were willing to spend time and money to make sure their relationship was real. In America, that is not exactly the business norm. Sure, a dinner here and there might be nice and a factory visit now and again might solidify the relationship, but it is still a work relationship. In China, it's more than that. That's why a person like Ning Yang is so vital to a cross-cultural company.

DAVE LANDIS
ENGINEER, SEMICONDUCTOR INDUSTRY

I relate to Ning Yang's story, and my experience is quite similar in some ways. In my case, I work with Chinese electrical engineers and mask designers in the semiconductor industry. A mask designer is a highly skilled technician who takes a schematic of a circuit and translates it into a physical representation using a library of cells. The engineering community is a mixture of Westerners, Indians, Chinese, and Vietnamese. The mask design community is comprised of a similar demographic, but the majority of these technicians are from China and Taiwan. The engineer is ultimately responsible for the work produced by the mask designer.

Mask designers were encouraged by their management to voice concerns and pinpoint inefficiencies that could impede project goals. I had the same management as the mask designers, so I knew that the desire to voice concerns was genuine. Amongst the mask designers from Taiwan and China, the tendency was not to voice concerns, even when management encouraged it. The prevailing attitude was to keep one's head low to avoid "gunfire." Westerners in the group would sometimes view this attitude as being somewhat "sheep-like." Nonetheless, these people were very diligent and hardworking.

I managed shared computer resources for a design team of about three hundred design engineers and mask designers at a high-tech company that was designing a very complex chip. Since there were multiple departments using a sizeable number of servers, it was imperative that the throughput be kept high and that idle server usage was to be discouraged. I wrote software to detect the idle computer usage of my colleagues. The software would e-mail the person wasting the resource, and if necessary, their manager. I would often follow up e-mails with either a phone call or a personal visit. On one occasion, I visited a Chinese colleague to explain to her that she was tying up a computer resource for a very long time and gave her an automated solution that would enable her to relinquish it when she left for the evening and obtain a new one just prior to her arriving the following morning. She was polite, but hesitant and resistant to this suggestion. After other similar conversations, I went to my management to get approval for some training time. The purpose of the training was not to single out any individual, but I sensed that my colleague was angry with me for making the presentation and took it personally.

Training sessions with the mask designers tended to be very quiet. No questions were asked publically, but it was not uncommon for them to stop by my office to ask questions on a personal basis or give me a phone call afterward.

So, just like this case scenario with Ning Yang, my suggestion is you meet with people one on one. In my case, I explained to my manager the cultural inhibitions that many Chinese would have in making public suggestions, and despite multiple exhortations to do so, they largely would stay quiet. One way that he would address this issue would be to make personal, informal visits to get a pulse on how things were progressing. These visits were non-threatening and since he was "the boss," there was a natural desire to provide good ideas.

Observations and Comments from Chinese Experts
SHOUZHENG (JEFFREY) CHENG
RUSSELL REYNOLDS ASSOCIATES, OPERATIONS MANAGER

In China, many Chinese think that Americans are weak in math, numbers, and calculations. We think that Americans don't like Excel and numbers. But we are wrong. It's true that Chinese are very strong in math and calculations. This is because of our solid foundation of math classes from the primary school. But Americans are much more skillful than many Chinese when it comes to using Excel and numbers to tell a story. For example, when I was at business school in the United States, I noticed that most of my American classmates liked working on Excel, especially in doing all kinds of different charts. Their presentations were full of numbers and facts that led them to their final conclusions. In this way, Americans are more number- and facts-focused than many Chinese.

Compared to the Americans, Chinese like using subjective and descriptive words in their presentations. In some Chinese companies, you see a lot of "polite and political, but useless" words during a presentation or speech. To illustrate this, allow me to play a "number game." Here is a comparison of a fifteen-minute presentation from an American company and a Chinese company. Below is the typical format:

American-Style Presentation

- Minutes 1–3: The purpose of this presentation and all possible solutions
- 4–10: Reasons behind those suggested solutions, using numbers, charts, and facts
- 11–12: Conclusion
- 13–15: Questions

Chinese-Style Presentation

- Minutes 1–2: "Thank-you letter" for this opportunity
- 3–10: Stories + some subjective opinions
- 11–13: Conclusion or explanation
- 14–15: "Thank-you letter" again + Questions

You can see the difference between these two presentation formats. Of course, today many Chinese companies are becoming more focused on facts and numbers, too, because they realize it is a better way to convince your audience.

As to my suggestions, if a Chinese company or employee wants to do business or make presentations to an American company, come prepared with all the facts and numbers that are related to your suggestions or conclusion. Americans always like asking this question: "SHOW ME THE NUMBERS!" Trust me, you will win the respect from your American colleagues if you have prepared answers that include facts and numbers.

DAJUN YANG
ALBERMARLE, CATALYST SALES MANAGER

Maybe, for the Americans, the focus is on the issue itself, but for Chinese, the issue often centers on human relationships. The problem-solving process may be pleasant for the Americans, but for most Chinese, it is a complicated system where we need to consider all types of human relationships. As such, here are some factors that influence what is perceived as "shy" performance.

First is the issue of face. For thousands of years, Chinese people have tried to avoid losing face, and everybody knows that we should not allow a Chinese person to lose face. For example, a father and son may have arguments in both Chinese and Western cultures. In the West, these conflicts may come from hurt feelings and disagreements; however, in China, one may even recognize his mistake, but because of face, he will not want to say that he is sorry. In this scenario, the manager who Jeff was dealing with may care a lot about face, and this could be why he doesn't want to confront the issue and have to admit that he was wrong. Jeff and Ning Yang did put a lot of effort into resolving the problem, and they did take him out to lunch on several occasions. It's always good to praise a person before blaming him. Try to acknowledge the good things that people do in management first. Say things like, "You are doing great in these areas, but it would be better to make improvements here." By talking in this way, Jeff and Ning Yang could have resolved the problem in one lunch.

Second, there is a deep-rooted sense of hierarchy. It should be stressed that, in the Chinese system, a person's lifelong career path can be damaged if he or she offends a superior along the way. In Western countries, without having to worry as much about face-saving issues, people can discuss problems directly, and this will not affect career development. Notice that the Western employees thought that their opinions would help in the HR meeting and would help management solve their problems. The Chinese employees were probably worried about whether or not their opinions would offend someone in human resources or make these people feel like they hadn't completed their job. These concerns are reasonable. Similar to the issue of losing face is the idea of retaliation. Of course, this is not an absolute, but there is a fear that if you cause someone to lose face, this person will make sure that you pay for it, too. In my own case, soon after graduation, I was working for a well-known American global consuming company. Once, in a staff meeting, I suggested an opinion that was different from the HR manager's. He retaliated by discrediting me in front of management whenever he got the chance to do so. As a recent graduate, I had no recourse to defend myself. In the end, I chose to leave the company because, after one year, I wasn't given any new training or development opportunities. Perhaps a solution to such a situation would be to get away from the one-on-one management and add a third person to the mix, such as a non-HR leader who can talk to the employees, too.

Perhaps I can illustrate this with a story from history. Shang Yang (*c.* 350 BC) was a statesman who assisted Qin's rise to power, extended his influence beyond the feudal states, and promoted the reunification. Before the reform, the first thing Shang Yang did was to gain the trust of the people. At the beginning of the reform, he put a thirty-foot log at the south gate of the capital, and he announced that if someone could move the log to the north gate that this person would receive ten gold pieces. Nobody trusted Shang Yang, so he increased the amount to fifty gold pieces. Someone moved the log to the north gate and, indeed, received the fifty gold pieces. With that, Shang Yang made it so that the people knew that he would do whatever he promised to do. If WEP could follow such a practice, I believe that people would speak their minds.

Finally, I should emphasize the importance of trust. In Chinese culture, people care about friends and loyalty. They only speak their minds to friends and people who they trust. This scenario provides a good example of this when Jeff received the license plate from the manager. That gesture demonstrated the sincere and warm heart that Chinese people have for their friends. Western culture relies more on regulations and rules, and this is improving gradually in China as well. But, still, in Chinese business collaboration, the focus on relationships is more important than the regulations and rules. I know of Chinese businessmen in Wenzhou who lend money to each other with no written agreements. They borrow large sums of money without contracts, and they return the money before the due dates. It may be hard for Western cultures to understand, but trust needs to be built over time. If they do not trust you, it really doesn't matter what you sign. There are reasons why you have to visit clients and have dinners and drinks together. In this scenario, the visa official must have wondered how he could trust someone who he had never met. It is true that Chinese people do not communicate as directly, especially when a conflict arises. Just follow their lead. If you use your heart to understand Chinese culture, your proposal will be implemented.

OLIVER HAN
AVARTO SERVICES, EXECUTIVE ASSISTANT TO THE VICE PRESIDENT

American colleagues, influenced by their traditional culture, usually show their opinions directly and openly, but Chinese are more reserved in this sense. We do not like direct confrontation, and this leads to different attitudes. Americans focus on things more than on people, and this brings about the results-oriented perspective, with people-issues being placed in a secondary position. I believe that Chinese focus on the people-factors first. Especially in state-owned companies, Chinese build human relationships first. After feeling comfortable with the people-issues, they can then focus on the other things. In China, we often hear, "When dealing with state-owned companies, deal with people first; when dealing with foreign companies, deal with things first." In this scenario, we see that the Chinese colleagues did not want to speak out directly at the meeting, but instead, they sent these ideas after the meeting. This is because they want to collaborate with the subcontractor.

Similar to the scenario, when I started working for an international company, it took me a while to get used to the American style of e-mails, which is totally different from a Chinese style. I would get e-mails that would say something like, "Please help finish xyz, and do 123 because we need abc." And then they would finally introduce themselves and sign the e-mail. At first, it made me feel weird, and I wondered why it was my job to do that. In China, the e-mail format would begin by introducing yourself and then you would write something like, "Hi, this is Joe, I'm working on abc project, and we are trying to do 123. We need your help to do xyz." Later, I noticed that this doesn't just apply to e-mails, but it also shows the different way that we talk, too. With that in mind, my recommendation is someone like the HR manager teach the Chinese employees about this "answer-first" approach and how effective it is.

Observations and Comments from the Authors

In some of the chapters of this book, the executive comments vary a lot. They may even contradict one another now and again. That is not the case in this chapter. It is significant to note that everyone focused on the importance that Chinese put on building personal relationships and giving face to others. In the case scenario itself, we see the word "face-to-face meeting," but the phrases "giving face" or "losing face" are not actually mentioned specifically. The executive comments, however, all picked up on this. Although many North Americans understand the concept behind giving and losing face, few actually feel the depth of the emotion. What we do see mentioned in the case is the need for direct communication, feedback, a discussion about the problems, and a focus on the issues. It is as Oliver Han mentioned: Americans focus on things; Chinese focus on people.

The mistake that many Americans make is to assume that the reason why Chinese do not offer their opinions is because they are disinterested, shy, or have no opinion. This is simply not the case. Dajun Han eluded in his comments that the Chinese have had thousands of years to work on avoiding losing face. Try to put yourself in the place of the Chinese. Consider for a moment how the comments during a group discussion could be construed. Everything that is said about human resources reflects on the HR manager. Everything that is said about the project design reflects on the project designers. Everything that is said about factory operations reflects on the factory supervisor, and everyone else involved with these operations, too. Chinese are so sensitive to the effects of avoiding the loss of face that even positive comments are seen in light of how those comments affect other people who are not the object of those comments. Dajun Yang even provided his own personal example of being discredited by a manager who had been offended by comments associated with a loss of face. No wonder it is easier to approach someone after the meeting to share ideas in private.

In looking at the American's tendency to focus on the issues and the Chinese tendency to focus on people, note that Arnold Pachtman's executive comments (even when addressing the issue of face and relationships) provide a bullet-point list of the "lessons" learned. Even here, he is addressing the issues. Dajun Yang, however, shares a 2,500-year-old story of the master statesman Shang Yang. No doubt, there are Western readers of this book who read the story and then wondered about the connection. Notice also that both Jeff Cheng and Oliver Han shared examples comparing the meeting and e-mail styles of the Americans and Chinese. The American style works because there is less of a need to be worried about face.

Sociologists often talk about a concept called "power distance," which refers to how much a subordinate may influence a superior. In some cultures (traditionally, for example, North American), the subordinates and the superiors almost see themselves as equals, which, in turn, makes it easier to share ideas and opinions. In other cultures (such as Chinese), traditional hierarchies put a greater distance between subordinates and superiors. In these cultures, there is almost a sense of "Why does he want my opinion? He is the boss, let him tell us what to do." In fact, a superior who has to ask the opinions of subordinates may even be perceived as a weak boss.

For readers who wish to discuss the topics in more depth, here are a few suggested questions:

1. Ning Yang notes that there is a younger generation of management teams that push to achieve international-standard certificates. How do the topics of building relationships and face tie into younger generation Chinese?

2. Magnus said that his wife, who is from Shanghai, agrees that a company would have to pay a premium to convince people to work in the second-tier cities. In terms of development and image, it is harder to convince people to live in other places. Is their any corollary with North American culture?

3. Many recommend that the solution to better communication with the Chinese is to meet with everyone in one-on-one situations. How realistic is that, however, and how can this advice be followed realistically?

4. Jeff Cheng observes that the Chinese are good at math, but the Americans are good at telling a story with numbers. What is he referring to?

5. How do you react to Oliver Han's comments about the style with which Americans and Chinese write e-mails. What do you do with this information?

6. Dajun Yang talks about how trust is a big part of building relationships, and the result is greater loyalty; however, in today's world, we see that many young executives easily switch from one job to another. How does one rectify this?

5

SORRY, WE DON'T HAVE THE BANDWIDTH

Company: IP Services

Focus: Experts in the testing and measurement of telecommunications equipment

Cultural Conflict: The Chinese market does not have a history of post-sale service; traditionally, business has been based on relationships rather than these types of warranties and agreements.

Introduction and Synopsis

IP Services is a multinational company that focuses on the testing of telecommunications equipment. In this scenario, Kai Wan, the senior regional sales manager, struggles with the difficult issue of extended warranties and post-sale service. Part of the difficulty revolves around the fact that, historically, Chinese companies were more accustomed to paying for things as they go. "If something doesn't break, leave it alone. If something breaks, fix it." Not all see the need for extended warranties, much less the cost of extended warranties. Part of Kai Wan's response has even been to conduct a number of seminars to teach about the benefits and cost savings associated with post-sales services. Of course, price is the bottom line, and a second challenge is his competitors will probably be selling extended warranties at a cheaper price. As he struggles to deal with these problems, things unfortunately coincide with the holiday season back at the home offices in Detroit. Consequently, this case also touches on communication with the home office and some of the challenges that come up there, too.

The executive comments after the case touch on the history of state-owned enterprises, the Chinese aversion to personal risk, and the importance of current price over future considerations. To be clear, all emphasize that it is not that the Chinese do not prepare for the future; it is more that things are changing very fast in China, and opportunities are centered on today and right now.

Finally, Kai Wan also talks about the benefits that come from having the Americans come to visit with the end-users in China. It helps to establish good relationships, and the Americans come away with a better sense of why the clients are reticent about the post-sale services.

Case Scenario

Kai Wan loves his job at IP Services, and he observes, "Have you noticed how bandwidth has become a new valid excuse for why we can't do something? Before we could blame time, money, or ability. But these three have now been joined by a new legitimate excuse: 'Sorry, but I don't have the bandwidth.'" As the senior regional sales manager of IP Services in Northern China and one who has been there for eight years, Kai Wan knows all about bandwidth. IP Services is a multinational company at the forefront of the testing and measurement of telecommunications equipment. The central offices are located in Detroit, but as Kai Wan says, IP Services is a very international company. "I work with Americans, Europeans, and Canadians. Our last VP was British, and our marketing VP was French. In Detroit, our factory manager is from Canada."

Given the nature of the high-tech world, however, where someone is from is secondary. The biggest challenge that IP Services faces everywhere in the world, including China, is to react in a timely manner to how technologies evolve, grow, and change. "We're all in a crunch to increase bandwidth," he adds. Between telecom operators and cable companies, IP (Internet protocol) networks have created a massive demand for high-speed technologies. Whether we are talking about voice-over IP; high-speed, content-rich Internet; or the dizzying numbers of megabits per second, the whole world is experiencing an explosion of applications and services. And this includes operations in over fifty countries where IP

Services has operations. China, understandably, has increasingly become one of IP Services' major areas of focus. The challenge is not even the end-user customer always understands the applications and services. "We not only have to sell our product to clients, but we have to explain to them what our applications and services are."

To provide some background, Kai Wan explains that IP Services has a country director in China, and the country has been divided into two major sections—north and south. Kai Wan is the sales manager of North China, putting him in charge of eighteen provinces. His responsibilities include working with four major telecom companies, which represent about 70 percent of his work. Beyond these telecom companies, his office also has contracts with several private, government, and military operations. One of his current projects is to work with a telecom company that will install operations in sixteen Chinese provinces. They will have over thirty branch offices in China, and installation of the new systems will be in sixteen of these offices. At this time, they are preparing the documents as well as getting ready for transmission testing, datacom testing, and optical line testing. IP Services does not perform the actual installation, but they are responsible for the selling and servicing of the products. The actual technical side of things, including testing, is going well. The problem Kai Wan is facing is related more to the fact that Chinese companies have little experience with the concept of post-sale servicing. The whole concept of guarantees and after-the-sale service is new to most Chinese.

For example, this Saturday Kai Wan hopes to have a teleconference with the factory director who is in Detroit. Usually Kai Wan does not have to worry about step-by-step approval from the home office, but this instance is unique. "We need approval from the Detroit offices because the financial details of a multi million dollar project that will have ramifications for our China offices for the next six years." The issue at hand is related to warranties and post-sale services. Right now, IP Services sells their product with a warranty for three years. Customers then have the option of extending their warranty for another three years. Their extended warranty costs about 20–24 percent of the list price of the original product (which is about 70 percent of the quoted price). Their fear is their competitor will offer post-sale services for about 5–7 percent of the list price. Kai Wan's proposal is to reduce the price of the extended warranty and post-sale services to about 5–10 of the original list price. So why is this also a cultural issue? First of all, Kai Wan explains that westerners are already used to the idea and value of post-sale services. "Here in China, it's still a relatively new concept. Most people think that it should be a free service." That is to say, most Chinese are of the mindset where if something breaks, you get it fixed, and if it doesn't break, leave it alone. For years, everything was owned by the state, and no one had the responsibility for maintenance or repairs. If there is no responsibility, there is no incentive to plan for future issues. Westerners, on the other hand, look at post-sale services similar to that of insurance. That is to say, there is a probability that something will happen, and based on that probability, people protect themselves with an extended warranty. In response to this, IP Services has conducted a number of training seminars for its Chinese customers. "We're trying to help people understand the benefits of post-sale extended services." IP Services has a program called Flexible Care in which they try to show how extended warranties actually help companies improve long-term budgeting because it helps them plan for future costs. Kai Wan thinks their efforts are paying off because the more value-added resellers relate to the financial benefits associated with extended warranties, the more willing they are to pay for them. "Chinese people don't normally think in those terms," adds Kai Wan. He explains that Americans are especially adept at planning for the future. If they know that they will need two of a given part every month, then they budget and plan for twenty-four parts during the whole year. In China, people tend to get things as they are needed. So if a company orders two of something today, they won't plan for the rest until it's needed. Maybe they'll order some more two weeks from now; maybe they'll order more two months from now. It's random and unplanned, and it clashes with the organized and budgeted way that Americans do things. As a sales manager, Kai Wan has to deal with this. The truth is his American colleagues do not understand why things can't be more structured and organized. So the conference call on Saturday isn't just to get permission to change the price of the extended service, it is also to help the home office understand why it's a difficult concept for their Chinese clients.

There is second issue that is related to Kai Wan's communications with the home office. In China, the months of November, December, and

January are key because people tend to try to get things done before the Chinese New Year (in February). Think of it like the end of the fiscal year for the U.S. government. "We try to complete our yearly purchases during that time. If we have budget items that have to be spent during the year, it is during this time that we need to take care of the year-end items." On the other hand, Americans are in more of a holiday and vacation mode during those months. For example, in preparation for Saturday's conference call, Kai Wan knows that his boss has been answering her e-mails from her Blackberry at home. Technically, she is on vacation, and Kai Wan hates to disturb her. On the other hand, he needs to get his work done. In her last response, she told him that he'd have an answer by Friday, but her Friday is his Saturday. Clearly, Kai Wan is nervous about this proposal and the implications it will bring for the next six years, an eternity for the high-tech industry.

Finally, there is also an issue of what it is like when the home office in Detroit sends representatives to visit China. "We need to show the Americans how local Chinese are reacting to our products and services." To do this, Kai Wan likes to take the Americans to visit the end-users. It's not enough to have meetings in the office. It helps to have them hear opinions about post-sale services directly from the Chinese clients. "Now, I realize that it is hard to get at what Chinese are really thinking," observes Kai Wan, "but it does help to have the Americans see the reticence that many Chinese express about the warranties and extended service." Part of the reticence stems from the fact that the end-users need to be reassured that even if a third party installs the product, IP Services will stand behind it. Once that is known, people are more willing to consider an extended warranty.

So good luck to Kai Wan this Saturday.

Observations and Comments from American Experts
ANDY FERGUSON
SOUTH MOUNTAIN CHINA TOURS, GENERAL MANAGER

As an executive who has worked in Asia and China for thirty years and who speaks Chinese fluently, I do consulting work for exactly the sorts of situations that Kai Wan finds himself in. Here's some advice that everyone in his and similar companies should pay careful attention to:

Kai Wan faces issues common to doing business in China with an "international" company based in the United States. In fact, IP Services is not an international company, but a U.S. company that sells its products internationally. If it were truly "international," then the decision-making authority for all sales in a market as important as China would be made by someone in China who deeply understands that market and has the authority to respond to the competition there.

Given the current state of the IP Services company, my guess is there is only one way Kai Wan can sleep soundly at night while he works there. He must have a VP for international sales in Detroit who everyone, including all the divisions in his company, are afraid of. Then that VP for international sales must support Kai Wan's decisions and defend him in the company. An important step toward true "international" status occurs when the company makes the "VP for international sales" or operations a required steppingstone for its highest executive position. The person in that position should have real international experience. When top bosses throughout the company know that the VP for International may soon be the big boss of the whole company, then they will pay attention to what he demands of them to meet international sales goals, and Kai Wan's job will then only be 300 percent more difficult than a U.S. manager of equal status, not 1,000 percent more difficult.

If, on the other hand, division and department heads and others are worried about overwhelming daily demands from people who call them on the phone during normal business hours (not international faxes sent because one party is too sleepy to talk coherently), then you've laid the foundation for failure.

Having said the above, which is critical, I'll mention a few ways Kai Wan can make things better for himself lacking a suitable VP angel to help him. First, Kai Wan's situation will be helped not only if he brings pertinent sales executives to China, but if he brings top-ranking engineers. When technical issues come up, it won't be enough to have sales executives batting for you at home; you must have the chief engineer on your side as well. Therefore, Kai Wan must bring top engineers to China, both to have them help sell products and also to gain an understanding and a personal investment in the customers' satisfaction. Again, if the chief engineer is more worried about a big U.S. customer who can yell at him on the phone each day instead of a distant voice in a faraway land, Kai Wan will never get the support he needs to succeed and grow long term.

There are several other things Kai Wan can do to help himself, but they should be obvious to anyone working in Asia. First, he must be totally familiar with his products and able to answer any possible technical questions his customers may have. It's likely that local conditions could create technical difficulties not found elsewhere, and these must be thoroughly understood and addressed by Kai Wan.

Kai Wan also needs to know his market niche well. One common problem in U.S. companies is that inexperienced executives from the home office don't understand that Asia is a competitive shark tank and a far more difficult place to do business than in the United States. Companies waste enormous amounts of time and money believing they can survive in the general market there. That's not usually the case. You must know exactly where your competitive strengths lie for the Asia market you're entering and concentrate heavily on those strengths. Growth then will usually come very slowly and depends highly on the growth of your main customers.

There's a lot more I can say, born of sometimes bitter experience, but this should give people food for thought.

James E. Satloff
Yellowstone Capital, Venture Partner

Kai Wan has his work cut out for him. Based upon my experience, both in the West and in Asia, Kai Wan's challenge is not in explaining the virtues of extended service contracts, and indeed, that may be his easiest task; his challenge is far more fundamental. Executives in America tend to have very different reasons for their actions than their counterparts in China. If the Chinese workers in question have a history working within state-owned enterprises (SOEs), as is often the case in the fields of telecommunications, such differences are even more acute. I acknowledge that many younger workers within China who have experience with foreign-owned companies tend to embody more of a combination of Chinese and Western business characteristics, but at the current time, they tend not to be the decision-makers in larger organizations.

It is precisely the notion of the responsibility of decision-making that drives much of the thought process of Chinese workers. When Kai Wan calls upon a company that has already decided to purchase IP Services' technology products, his counterparty will almost certainly not be the person who made that decision. Historically, it will have been a very senior executive, and it will be the balance of the executives that will be charged with executing (to the letter) the tasks required to comply with the agreement. Kai Wan will be wasting his breath trying to convince his clients' executives to add the extended warranty to their contract. For those executives, there is simply no incentive to do so. In the West, even a somewhat senior-level manager will be incented by one or more of the following possibilities: a) standing out from his peers, b) monetary bonuses or performance-related compensation, and/or c) risk-taking. In China, these possibilities are generally avoided. Kai Wan's client will not wish to take the risk of purchasing the extended service. The Chinese counterparty will be thinking such varied thoughts as the following:

- Why should I authorize spending my employer's money now for something that may never happen?
- If service is needed three years from now, I might not even be here.
- If the company saves money in three years because it purchased the extended service, who will even know that it is because of my decision?
- If I send this purchase requisition to our executive committee, they will ask why I am requesting this, and they might ask me this question in front of my peers, which will be embarrassing for me.
- There would be no reward for me to take such a risk as to commit money now for something so far in the future.
- If IP Services is such a good company, why does it cost so much for service so far in the future? Do they believe that their products and services will break or fail? I do not wish to be associated with this.
- Why is Kai Wan putting me in such an awkward position? The extended service contract should have been agreed on by our executive committee when they agreed to buy the services in the first place.

Kai Wan also has the problem of explaining these cultural differences to his Detroit colleagues. For most Westerners, standing out for taking risks and peaking one's mind and respectfully giving various opinions on a business decision is not only commonplace, it is expected of most employees. "Don't stand out; you might be fired. Don't take a risk; you might be wrong. Don't offer your opinion unless you are asked; you might embarrass your manager. Don't ask any questions until your manager asks if you have any." These are the thoughts that go through the mind of many employees of Chinese SOEs. Kai Wan's colleagues in the States will think that he is kidding them, but he is not.

As to my recommendation, Kai Wan would be best served by describing the different mindset of Chinese workers compared with Western workers and pointing out that, for smaller, foreign-funded or private-funded companies, employees are more likely to have Western-style mindsets about business. If he is successful in conveying this concept to Detroit, he should urge his product-development team to segment the market and create two different tiers of service. Those two tiers would be the extended warranty service, as presented in the case, but the second would be a pay-as-you-go option, where clients could purchase the service from IP Services on an as-needed basis, but the prices for such services are established today, for the twelve-month period three years from now. Each year, the price schedule for three years from now would be provided to clients. In this way, a company would know what it will cost for a specific service three years from now, and IP Services can be viewed as being very respectful of its clients in China by committing now to a menu of services and associated pricing, without requiring the commitment of the client today. Naturally, it will be more costly than the first option, but this will be easily understood and appreciated by clients. Kai Wan will quickly discern during his client meetings which type of client he is facing. The more established and state-owned enterprises will likely opt for the second option and will view it as a strong partnership. (Indeed, that would be an excellent way for Kai Wan to pitch the idea.) Newer, smaller, or foreign- or private-invested companies could be actively pitched with the prepaid extended warranty. He will not have difficulty explaining to Detroit that Chinese companies will already expect IP Services to stand behind its products and solutions, but Kai Wan may have difficulty explaining to his American colleagues that when they are in front of Chinese clients, those clients are very likely not to be particularly forthcoming about flaws in IP Services' products or solutions. After a short period of incredulity, his colleagues will see that he is probably correct, and at the very least, his approach would not introduce much risk. Having the meeting on Saturday may be a stroke of luck, as the Americans will be forced to have a day or two to think about things rather than responding with the immediate, gut feeling that so many American managers do. Good luck, indeed, to Kai Wan.

MAGNUS & MINGXING LARSEN
MANDMX.COM, FOUNDERS AND CREATORS

First, Kai Wan wants to reduce the price of the post-sale services mainly because the Chinese don't really understand this idea. The American boss will not go for this. There will be questions about why the Chinese don't understand the post-sale services, and it will be clear that Kai Wan has not effectively communicated the ideas and benefits to the Chinese bosses about those benefits. This scenario mentioned that there have been seminars that properly communicate the good points of warranties, and as a result, many of the Chinese clients do purchase the post-sale services. Kai Wan's boss will tell Kai Wan to work overtime to get those seminars to the bosses before he lowers the price. We think Kai Wan should do everything at his disposal (e.g., conduct seminars, visit the clients) before he attempts to lower the cost of his company's product.

Second, the point that Kai Wan makes is a fascinating one: "Americans are especially adept at planning for the future and Chinese are not." Thus, we see, for example, the fact that Costco is a booming business in America where people can buy in bulk, but it is not a booming business in China. Any visitor to China won't necessarily see that Chinese don't plan for the future, but if a Westerner has lived in China for a number of years, it will become apparent. (This is especially true if you are married to a Chinese). At Costco, you buy in bulk, and in China, you go to the local market and buy only food for tonight's dinner. Another example of this is the way we look at funerals. Most Americans don't enjoy planning for the death of a loved one, but they know that it is a fact of life. Drawing up a last will and testament is something that is considered to be a bit morbid but necessary to not cause problems in the future. Bring this up to a Chinese family member about middle-aged or elderly parents and that person would be shunned, shushed, or even thrown out of the house. Even after five thousand years of life and death, death is still a taboo topic. Thus, many families that I've known have problems with estates and money when the elderly do pass away, and it causes major problems within the family. For many years, my parents have told me that their last will and testament is all done and ready and that they've even purchased their plot of land in the cemetery. When I told my wife, a Shanghainese, she was shocked. The American boss and management in this case scenario won't understand this right away, and it depends on Kai Wan's ability to explain this particular cultural item. Our opinion is that this issue isn't the same as death, but it is about the future and good business sense, and Kai Wan needs to explain this to the clients. Chinese don't like to think about the future, but they do like to save money, and if Kai Wan can persuade the clients that this is about saving money and not about bringing bad luck, he will please his boss.

Third is the question of communicating with the home office. This only takes communicating before everything starts up. Both parties need to be clear about which time of the year is busy and which is not. I know many people who don't know much about China will complain that, when doing business with China, you have to be careful because there are so many holidays. You never know if there is going to be some national holiday or some local holiday when nobody will be in the office. This, of course, is not necessarily true. Perhaps this is a convenient excuse coming from China, similar to the "low bandwidth" excuse. Not only is the timing for communication very important, but it's also essential for both parties to understand the time zone of all countries involved. So when the boss says that they will get back to Kai Wan on Friday, they need to be clear whether it's their Friday or China's Friday. This all takes communication and perhaps a third party to help their company understand these issues and teach personnel from both countries. Or a book like this one would be helpful, too, for both parties involved.

Observations and Comments from Chinese Experts
JIAHAI (JOHN) ZHANG
PANDA EXPRESS, AREA COACH HONOLULU

I really relate to Kai Wan's situation. China has a totally different culture toward post-sale service. Traditionally, Chinese companies and end-users are accustomed to free service for the products they buy or for the services they pay for. They normally haven't looked at purchases with long-term planning. The assumption has always been that if a product is any good, it shouldn't need an extended warranty. Also, if Chinese did buy a warranty, they would worry about if the company would still be there to provide a future service. This is all related to what Chinese end-users think of companies and products.

In some ways, Kai Wan probably should have been more proactive with his work in his home office. Since he knew that Chinese try to get things done before the Chinese New Year and that his boss would be spending the holidays in December at home, he should have planned his work earlier. I do agree with Kai Wan's proposal to reduce the price of the extended warranty and the post-sale services to about 5–10 percent of the original list price. That way, it will be much easier for Chinese to try the benefit of post-sale service. Once they experience the benefits, they will continue to buy other warranties in the future, and they will share those opinions with their friends.

I also thought that it was a good idea to take the Americans to visit the end-users in China. This could have been done a long time ago. I believe this is related to understanding one another's culture. It makes everybody's job much easier. This is also part of Kai Wan's potential proactive activities in helping his boss understand Chinese culture.

As to the conference call on Saturday, Kai Wan should apologize to everyone that he didn't get the job done on time. He really needs to let everyone understand Chinese culture and his present situation. Then he should present his action plan, which actually sounds pretty good. Then he can be humble and listen to other good suggestions from the others. In my own case, our company is also mixed with American and Chinese culture, and it is good for business when we have different opinions. We learn a lot from each other. It is a challenge for everyone to do things in a way that benefits everyone else. The main thing is trying to understand each other.

DAJUN YANG
ALBERMARLE, CATALYST SALES MANAGER

There are many subtle cultural reasons why people have different ideas about post-sale services, but it is wrong to say that there is no post-sale service history in China. When I was little, I remember a popular commercial that advertised a product that was "durable and with three guarantees." The three guarantees were a guarantee to repair, to exchange, or to return. The law stipulates that the post-sale services are the responsibility of the manufacturer; therefore, the focus on this case is really more in the area of extended warranties.

Before the reform and opening up of China, all enterprises (e.g., factories, schools, hospitals, and radio and TV stations) were state-owned. If some electrical appliance broke down, it was easy to find some skilled person to help with the problem within the enterprise. Although some companies offered services, they seldom took on the responsibility of post-sale service. After China's reform and opening, a new market economy system was started, and state-owned enterprises are not a major part of the economy anymore. Those that were responsible for post-sale services disappeared. Chinese people cannot solve problems within the enterprises anymore.

The problem that Kai Wan encountered was not just related to cultural difference, but also market ones. And it looks like Kai Wan hasn't found the key to the problem. He thought Western people care more about future planning, while Chinese focus just on what they need currently. It may be more related to the fact that Chinese people believe that they can buy what they need whenever they need it. I think Kai Wan should first explain that Chinese people do acknowledge the need for extended warranties, but that they need to adjust their understanding of how they are formatted. Second, during negotiation, they need to focus on price and put less emphasis on the reduction of services. At the same time, he should explain to the home office that there are aspects of China being a developing market, and things will not necessarily work the same.

I currently work for a fine U.S. chemical company and am responsible for a catalyst products business in China, including dangerous goods. In the United States and Europe, we provide paid security training and technical services, which do not work as well in China. Rather than charge for the training in China, our strategy is to show them our experience in dealing with the safety issues, fires, and levels of risk through photos, videos, and fire drills. We do not charge them for this, but after they know us better, we then sell better service at a higher price. Currently, the market recognizes our higher price because we provide additional services. We did not try to change the deep-rooted ideas that Chinese have, but instead, we used known methods and price to get us started and then introduce paid services at the proper time. We also communicate with the home office to help them understand the current market in China. Kai Wan is facing some of these same issues.

A brief word about vacations and holidays—under fierce market competitions, if you do not work during holidays or put in overtime, somebody else will. The boss will surely prefer the person who is willing to do so. Although new labor laws have been introduced into China, it takes time to show changes. In my own case, I work for an American company, and I have the same problems during the final quarter of each year. I usually visit with clients during the holidays. Then what I usually do is ask the American colleagues at home whether it is OK to contact them during the holidays. I make it their choice.

ZHEN (STEVE) YANG
DELOITTE, SENIOR CONSULTANT

More than just differences in cultural conflicts, this case is a good example of the differences in the business environment. Most Chinese consumers are aware of post-sale service and recognize its value; however, in some industries, post-sale service is a different story. Unfortunately, telecom is one of those industries. Historically, the China telecom has been monopolized by three large state-owned enterprises. All the multinational and local telecom equipment providers compete to get contracts from these three telecom companies. The basic principle is you sell the equipment to telecom companies, make sure the equipment works well, build the relationship with the clients, and get new contracts. If something goes wrong with your equipment, you are out of the market. Post-sale service becomes more important for companies like IP Services, but less so for the China telecom companies. In order to get new contracts, most companies are willing to provide post-sale service for free or for just a small fee to cover the basic expenses. I believe that it is Kai Wan's responsibility to clarify the difference in the Chinese business environment and to adjust their policy to adapt to that difference. If the company just copies their U.S. strategy, they will definitely fail in this market.

It is interesting to see that Westerners sometimes complain that the Chinese do not have a plan for future purchases. Actually, Chinese companies do plan for their activities, but often, rapid economy development causes more radical changes than expected. Sometimes the employees in state-owned enterprises are not sophisticated enough to understand these changes. The truth is this challenge also creates opportunities for companies. If a company keeps up with the market, actively interacts with the clients, and helps them to understand the problem and solutions, it will definitely become a winner in the market. For example, in my experience, we actually forecasted trends for our clients, we educated them on the need for new equipment, and we planned our production according to those forecasts. As a result, the needed purchases seldom became surprises. However, if a company just waits for the clients to knock on the door, it might as well consider quitting the China market.

Finally, let me make one observation about Chinese New Year. The time before Chinese New Year is key to building relationships and securing contracts. Considering the time differences and the Western holiday season, it would be better if the U.S. parent company were to give the employees in China more power and flexibility to make the decisions rather than wait for the decision from headquarters every time. When entering into the China market, the company must understand the differences in the industry and the business environment and define their new strategy that will be fit for both the company and this market.

Observations and Comments from the Authors

This chapter seems to have an underlying theme of how tradition and innovation have to balance each other out. On one end, we see a China that is reacting fast to new technologies, new growth, and rapid change. On the other end, we see how patterns from the traditional state-owned enterprises are striving to adjust to new market realities. This case deals with telecommunications, the perfect example of where these two extremes meet. The issue of extended warranties falls right in the middle these two extremes. To understand the cultural part of this, it is helpful to draw from some of the models that exist in intercultural communications. For example, Hofstede's famous cultural dimensions include a category called "uncertainty avoidance." Some cultures are OK with working with unknown, unstructured situations, with taking risks, and with letting the future take care of itself. At first glance, one would think that the aversion to risk that we see among the Chinese is related to their uncertainty avoidance. Ironically, however, Hofstede's index for uncertainty avoidance between China and the United States is not all that different. Instead, what we see happening, as Kai Wan himself explains, is that things are developing so fast that not even the end-users always understand the applications and services. No wonder James Satloff warns that Kai Wan's colleagues in the United States will think that he is kidding, but he is not.

Note that many of the executives who comment on this case try to place the context within the historical perspective of what it meant to have state-owned enterprises. It is not so much that Chinese do not worry about the future, it is more related to whose responsibility it was to deal with changes. As mentioned, if the decision-makers are the older, senior-level executives, those who come from state-owned enterprise backgrounds, a demonstration on the cost savings will do more than an emphasis on the future or risks.

A second cultural issue that comes out in this case is that of time zones, calendars, holidays, and vacations. Do not minimize the importance of being sensitive to holidays. Our experience is that North Americans relate to how hard it would be to gather certain data between December 23 and January 1. Unfortunately, many do not transpose that feeling to how difficult it is for other cultures to do similar work during their holidays. Indeed, many Chinese are willing to work extra hours and on holidays, too. However, their interaction with local contacts becomes extremely limited during vacation times (e.g., Chinese New Year). This is partly the reason why Steve Yang suggested that companies give Chinese more power to make decisions locally. It is also the reason why Andy Ferguson suggested that a VP for international sales be in place as well.

This case brings up several potential topics for further discussion. Interested readers may want to consider the following:

1. What do you think of James Satloff's suggestion to create a two-tier system where a second possibility would be to have a pay-as-you-go option by which the clients would purchase the post-sale services on an as-needed basis?

2. Magnus Larsen uses the example of buying in bulk versus buying for tomorrow and the aversion to planning in advance for funerals.

In what way do you agree or disagree that these examples represent Chinese focus on the current moment versus the future?

3. Andy Ferguson's observation is IP Services is not an international company, but really more of a U.S. company that sells their products internationally. He goes on to say that to be truly international, the decision-making for China would need to be made by people in China. In what ways is this a matter of size and resources versus a matter of focus? What other factors might come into play?

4. John Zhang says that Chinese have always worked under the assumption that if a product is good, it shouldn't need an extended warranty. He also observed that even if companies had a warranty, chances are they would worry about if the company would still be around in the future to provide the service. How do you respond to these observations?

5. James Satloff says that it is precisely the notion of responsibility of decision-making that drives much of the thought process of Chinese workers. He also notes that the person who Kai Wan will deal with to purchase services from IP Services will not be the person who had the authority to make the initial decision. Do you agree, and how does one respond?

6. What strategies are there to work around national holidays and vacations? Steve Yang mentions that the time just before Chinese New Year is a key moment to build relationships and secure contracts. What could he be referring to?

6

IF YOU MAKE A PROMISE, KEEP IT

Company: Aircargo West
Focus: Increased activity in the air cargo industry, both in and out of China
Cultural Conflict: It is important to time to build relationships, especially as it applies to working with people who work for state-owned enterprises

Introduction and Synopsis

In this scenario, as Ray Brimble mentions in his executive comments, old-school courtesy with a focus on people is not dead. Jie Lo is in his sixties now, and he has that distinguished look of a confident professional. He genuinely enjoys people and is comfortable talking to high-level executives and government officials, but he is also at ease with the common laborers. It is always a delight to meet people who have gone through life with a sense of gratitude, and that is the impression you get of Jie Lo. And he is a tireless worker, or as he puts it, "I'm on my blackberry twenty-four hours a day. Why make that other person wait for the information?" Jie Lo works for Aircargo West Airlines, and with all of the increased exports that leave China, there is a continual adjustment to the flight schedules of the planes that come and go in and out of China. In order to make these adjustments, Jie Lo spends a lot of time talking to government officials to approve the new flights. As you talk to Jie Lo, you get a sense of what an asset he is for Aircargo—a man who has made forty years of connections, a native speaker of Cantonese and Mandarin, and a person who fully understands the party system and the layers of bureaucracy in the state-owned enterprises. His secret? Jie Lo knows that Americans might minimize it, but there is a lot of work that goes into building relationships. In all his years, he has never paid any money under the table because he has learned that things happen on friendship, which he keeps alive and growing.

After reading the case, readers will note that the executive comments focus on the same ideas. Roger Sun is the lone exception who feels that building relationships in China is no different than building relationships anywhere else in the world. But the vast majority confirms that people are important. Additionally, in China, especially in the state-owned enterprises, one needs to know the role of the CEO and the party secretary. In Chris Li's comments, he summarizes the idea that in order to work together, Chinese need to build trust, as opposed to Americans who trust everyone until given a reason not to. As the title of this case suggests, if you make a promise, keep it.

Case Scenario

Jie Lo was born and raised in Hong Kong but moved to the United States in 1974. He graduated from the University of Chicago Graduate School of Business, then moved to New York, where he began working for Aircargo West Airlines, a company that he has been loyal to for nearly forty years. Currently, he is the managing director for Greater China and Southeast Asia, and his main role is that of opening up air cargo opportunities in China, both in the mainland as well as in Hong Kong. This implies that he spends a good portion of his time talking to professional and government officials in order to secure approval for new flights, destinations, and schedules. Given the increasing number of companies that are moving to China and the great number of factories that are shifting to Asia, it stands to reason that freight-forwarding companies are going to have to figure out how to increase entry into China. This also implies, in addition to increased entry, that companies will also be shipping more finished goods out of China as well. Jie Lo knows that all of this means that Aircargo West needs to work hard to increase its presence. "We have to build our gateways into China, especially in Shanghai, Beijing, and Guangzhou," he adds. "But we also have to increase capacity, staff, and equipment. Just this year, we tripled the number of flights to China!" This includes an increased need for the A380 super jumbo aircraft as well as the B747 freighter aircraft. During the past year, Jie Lo has seen new connections between Shanghai and Anchorage as well as additional flights into Los Angeles and then on to other hubs around the country.

Jie Lo's first observation about working with Americans and Chinese is how the Americans do not understand how state-owned businesses are run in China. "One of the problems is that American CEOs are not always aware of the role of party secretaries in China." In private companies, things are not so different from Western standards; however, although state-owned companies are lead by a CEO (who also has to be a Communist Party member), the party secretary holds a major position on the board of directors. The party secretary is directly appointed by the politburo of the Communist Party. It becomes his job to make sure that governmental policies are followed. Even positive responses from CEOs are temporary in China. Everything needs to pass through the influence of the party secretaries. "So," as Jie Lo explains, "not only do Americans have a hard time understanding the role of the CEO versus the party secretary, but they also do not understand that, in China, the higher one's position is, the less he will have control of his schedule." For example, Jie Lo recently made an appointment for an American CEO to meet with a high-ranking party secretary in Beijing. The meeting was scheduled for 10:00 a.m., but at the last moment, the Chinese official was called away. The American CEO was quite put out. It was clear that he wasn't used to being bumped, especially when taking the extra time to travel halfway around the world to conduct business. Jie Lo had to tell him to be patient because, "in China, government issues always take priority over business issues." Important people need to take care of emergencies and official business. In this instance, the Chinese official was able to meet with the American CEO that same afternoon, and in the end, everything turned out just fine. The point, however, is the party secretary had less flexibility in controlling his schedule than what the American appreciated.

Jie Lo notes a similar instance not too long ago when another American businessman had scheduled a dinner with a different party secretary. In the middle of the dinner, the party secretary had to leave to go talk to some other people for a while. Of course, he did leave some other representatives from the Chinese company with the American. The American mentioned to Jie Lo how rude it was of the party secretary to leave like that. About an hour later, the party secretary came back and finished the dinner. "I had to explain to the American CEO that, if anything, this man was showing him a great sign of respect." The party secretary had begun and ended the dinner with him. "Everyone else who the party secretary had visited only got a visit in the middle of their events." Jie Lo isn't sure that the American ever fully appreciated what it meant to have the party secretary spend as much time as he did with the American visitor.

"You know," adds Jie Lo, "here in China, things happen purely on friendship. It has always been a matter of building friendships." Many suppose that Jie Lo has had to pay something under the table to get things done. But he is quick to assure you that, in over thirty years of working with the Chinese, he has never had to do so. "If you don't build friendships, all you will ever hear is how sorry people are that things can't get done." At the same time, Jie Lo adds that building friendships requires a lot work. Recently, there was an American acquaintance who told Jie Lo that he worked too hard. "I told him no. If somebody needs information, I will pass it on to him as soon as I can. I'm on my Blackberry twenty-four hours a day. Why make that other person wait for the information?" And that is the attitude that Jie Lo carries with him when it comes to building friendships. "This isn't just for business professionals," adds Jie Lo. "Government people in Washington don't understand this, either." In fact, he hates to say it, but the word that best describes Americans in this sense is "naive." They just don't realize how much work goes into building friendships.

For example, Jie Lo reminds people that, in China, you need to talk to managers at all levels to find out their style and their strengths and weaknesses. "If you don't do this, people at lower levels will say that nobody told them to do things." Even if a senior executive approves something, the mid-level person won't follow through without direct permission. Jie Lo suggests that you talk to everyone at all levels. Let the senior know that you'll be talking to the mid-level person directly. That way, everyone knows what is going on and things can get done. "Like I said, building friendships is hard work."

Jie Lo offers another example to show the importance of building friendships. He remembers one time when two large high-tech companies sent senior representatives to China in preparation for a gigantic project where they would be designing and providing airport equipment that would be used in Chinese airports. Initially, the first phase was a $29 million deal. In true Chinese style, the Chinese treated the American visitors well. This included the use of a private jet, taking them out to nice dinners, showing them around, and all the other aspects of special Chinese treatment. Anyone who has been a recipient of this treatment will have an idea of how intense it is. The Americans seemed genuinely impressed by the Chinese generosity and friendship. They even said, "OK, next time you are in the United States, I'll fly you out, and we can meet and talk some more." Since that was the way that they had been treating the Americans, they thought that would be fine. Later, when some of these Chinese executives were in the United States, they stopped in Denver to visit with these senior representatives. At the end of dinner, because there were eight Chinese and only two Americans, the Americans suggested that they split the bill 50/50. The Chinese were shocked. How is it possible, considering that they had begun with a $29 million deal, and remembering the way they had treated the Americans while in China, that now they wanted to split the bill for dinner? "In the end," adds Jie Lo, "they respected the initial $29 million obligation, but they never renewed business with them." In essence, they lost out on a multimillion-dollar operation because they were too cheap to pay for dinner. Clearly, this was just a misunderstanding. But the Chinese were looking at this as an issue of personal integrity. "We don't want hollow promises," Jie Lo repeated. "When you build a working relationship, if you make a promise, you have to keep it." He also reiterates that Americans are generally thought of a people who are easy to get to know. "But they are harder to get along with as time goes by." They give the impression initially that they are going to build friendships, but it often dies out along the way.

On the positive side, Jie Lo has had the opposite experience as well. "I had a mentor, an American, at a previous position where the company was going through a financial crisis." When problems arise, senior managers often act like they don't know what is happening, but this mentor was different. Although his job and future options were protected, he helped Jie Lo analyze his options. "A number of companies were looking at me, and my mentor gave me advice and help." In the end, Jie Lo was able to negotiate a good career move with a new company—Aircargo West, in fact. "My mentor simply didn't allow me to make a bad decision." Even today, almost thirty years later, Jie Lo knows that the thing that matters most is trust. "It's an honor to have known this person, and it has influenced how I have conducted business as well."

So, now, Jie Lo finds himself as busy as ever. In the next few weeks, he needs to solidify how some new flights will be routed. "The aircargo industry is impressive," he adds. "You have to coordinate the aircraft, the timing of the connecting flights, the freight booking, and the inspections, loading, storage, and overland transportation of the cargo." It's a good thing that he has built solid friendships along the way.

Observations and Comments from American Experts

RAYMOND J. BRIMBLE

LYNXS GROUP, PRESIDENT AND CEO

Jie Lo reminds us that "old school" is not dead. Being a fellow aviation industry person, I realize how much government still dominates decision-making in this space, not just in China, but in all over the world. This fact dominates Jie Lo's perspective but does not diminish his observations that Americans must consider the effects of working with state-owned businesses. Chinese commercial growth gives many Americans the impression that capitalism has triumphed. But in the discussion of the air cargo industry, Jie Lo reminds us that the commissariat is alive and well, and even the CEO has to answer to the party in the end (at least for the time being).

Jie Lo goes on to describe two instances wherein a Chinese CEO is "called away" in one and Americans are bad dinner hosts in another. Jie Lo is right about how irritated Americans get when top executives are constantly called away. This is almost a ritualistic affair, and Americans have little sympathy for it, no matter what the reason. It speaks to a lack of focus, and the impression Americans always have is that they have come halfway around the world and the least their hosts could do is give them a few contiguous hours together without being "called away." The sheer frequency of this happening makes most American businesspeople wary. In my experience, it really is quite typical.

The second instance regarding the American dinner hosts who wanted to split the check 50/50 is simply outrageous and rude in any culture. If these Americans were so insensitive to their guests to have suggested such a thing, well, they should be taken off the project. This sort of behavior is not typical for American hosts. The bottom line is if the Americans do not feel they can justify a dinner tab, then they probably cannot endure nor afford the investment in time, money, and energy that is required to launch a successful venture in China. My advice to their Chinese counterparts would be to "run for your lives" and find another American business partner!

Finally, getting back to "old school," I have noticed a distinct rift in the business styles of older businesspeople and the younger school, not only in China, but across the world. Friendships are always important, not just in China. But the emphasis of "purely" personal relationships, and the long process of building them, is both a credit to the Jie Lo's focus and also an indicator of his style as much as his substance. I suspect that younger businesspeople on both sides of the Pacific may naturally gravitate to a seemingly speedier style of business development. At the same time, I doubt that this increased rapidity will be any more effective than Jie Lo's "old school" style.

A.J. WARNER
MBATOUCHDOWN.COM, PRESIDENT

China has historically been a very hierarchical society. This remains true today in the Chinese government and businesses, even in subsidiaries of U.S. companies operating in China. American businesspeople, in general, feel uncomfortable about hierarchy due to our education and lack of experience working in such strict environments. Combine this with the fact that China's companies are very political in nature. The HR department is often one of the most powerful departments in the entire company, which is very different compared to the United States. Within companies, a political wing links the company directly to the Chinese government. The employees in these political roles work for both the company and the state. They are very powerful within the company even though they are not directly involved in the company's operations. It is important for American businesspeople to recognize that Chinese state-owned companies have political responsibilities. Chinese companies focus on how they can help the state itself, while U.S. companies focus only on the company's bottom line. From the American perspective, this seems strange, but from the Chinese side, it seems natural and patriotic.

The point about not getting any additional contracts after the initial $29 million contract is interesting. This incident reveals how cultural differences create unfortunate misunderstandings between people. From my experiences in working with Chinese businesspeople, they do not personally have to pay any expenses. It is accepted as a major part of doing business. Chinese firms are not strict at all about reimbursement. In fact, their entertainment budgets typically are proportionately huge compared to U.S. companies. In fact, a large part of business in China is conducted at restaurants in the evening, not in meeting rooms during the day. On the other hand, U.S. companies place strict restrictions on what can and cannot be reimbursed. I feel that Chinese companies would have a difficult time succeeding in business if they were managed by the same set of strict rules that face American businesspeople when trying to compete in business. In the story, the Americans do not get a contract extension due to being "cheap" while entertaining a group of Chinese who were visiting the United States. Jie Lo identified the outcome but did not try to understand why the Americans reacted differently than what he assumed they should. When the Americans asked to split the dinner bill, they probably worried about their boss's displeasure about the high expense of entertaining the Chinese visitors. In fact, they probably were worrying whether their company's rules would allow reimbursement of the expense.

From the Chinese standpoint, they assume that the expense will be taken care of by the company. They do not understand the complicated rules in U.S. companies about expenses. Their displeasure at being asked to pay is directed at the company, which is supposed to pay for their dinner, but fails to understand the human side of the situation. Personally, when I was a young employee, I was asked to entertain some clients who were attending the Consumer Electronics Show (CES) in Las Vegas while my boss entertained more important clients. What was supposed to be a few drinks with three buyers turned into a nearly $2,000 entertainment expense. Although my customers were happy with my company, my boss was very upset. I remember worrying that I would not be reimbursed. That was my whole net income for the month at that time. In the end, I got the reimbursement, but I will never forgot the feeling of worry. On the surface, the American businesspeople should have paid for the dinner, but I feel that the sense of worry due to U.S. business practices was a major influence on the resulting loss of the major contract.

My recommendation for American businesspeople is to discuss the need for entertainment expenses when working with Chinese clients. The American businesspeople need more flexibility from their headquarters to be effective. In addition, U.S. companies need to recognize that Chinese decision-making is slower, often, on purpose, so business trips need to be more flexible and maybe even longer. In fact, by being slow, the Chinese gain an advantage over their U.S. counterparts who feel a great sense of urgency to sign a deal, even if it is not in their best interest, because they need to justify the trip to China. U.S. businesspeople need to watch for this common mistake when negotiating with Chinese businesspeople.

KAREN BOYER
GOODWILL INDUSTRIES OF CENTRAL TEXAS, SPECIAL EVENTS COORDINATOR

The generosity I witnessed in China often amazed me. It seemed to be a regular thing for friends to lend each other cars or thousands of Chinese RMB. If someone was in need, everyone chipped in to help, whether it was a business or a personal relationship. People were generous with both time and money. It was taken for granted that if a close friend or colleague asked you for help, you would drop everything to do so. Sometimes, it meant leaving dinners halfway through or cancelling appointments; however, since everyone there understands the culture, no one complains—at least not too much.

One time that this generosity was visible was when a colleague of mine arranged a lunch for us with some local government officials. After lunch, I was invited to go to a local park with the group but declined, as I was moving the next day and needed to finish packing up my apartment. On the way home, I asked if they would drop me off at a local store, instead of my home, so I could pick up some more boxes. The official took the opportunity to show me his generosity by having his subordinates bring boxes to my apartment and pack everything for me. The people who worked for him really didn't have any choice when he called. They had to stop what they were doing and come help me. This often happens with government workers. Everyone has someone above him or her who may be trying to start or maintain a useful relationship. In order to do this successfully, they utilize the efforts of their subordinates. Although the government official was very kind to help me, he was also starting a relationship where he could seek advice on Western cultures when needed.

The flip side of the coin may be that you have an appointment that is cancelled or delayed at the last minute. The same government official who facilitated the packing of my apartment also had to cancel or delay some of our future appointments to tend to something for his superior. Government business always takes priority in his life.

There is a hierarchy of relationships that can affect your work in China. The situation above illustrates two types. One is a lateral relationship among friends or business acquaintances that are friends. This is the type of situation that existed between the government official and I. This usually involves a lot of generosity in time, money, or both. Someone who is a friend and a business partner would come before someone who is just a business partner. The other situation illustrated above is more of a vertical relationship. This is similar to that of the government official and those who worked for him. When someone who is above you asks for help, there is often no choice but to stop what you are doing and help. This often, for example, implies the need to cancel or reschedule important business appointments. For many Westerners, this can be very frustrating. When dealing with government officials, showing your understanding of the requirements of their position will help your relationship. If possible, have a local person guide you through the intricacies.

Observations and Comments from Chinese Experts

WEIMIN CHEN
GREATER CHINA HQ, CHANNEL OPERATIONS MANAGER

When I read this case, the first thought that came to mind was that "building relationships" might have a different meaning for Americans and Chinese. For Americans, this means more of a business relationship, but for Chinese, it means more of a personal friendship.

Building relationships with customers may not be more important than products and service, but they are also no less important for a company that is doing business in China. For American companies in China, although most of the top managements are from Hong Kong, Taiwan, Singapore, etc., most of the sales directors and managers are local people who have established relationships and even better communication skills with the customers. They work on a daily basis with customers and are experienced in dealing with customer issues. In my company, our major customers are state-owned banks, insurance companies, telecommunication companies, and government institutes. The CEOs of these customers are not only the leaders of the business units, but they also play important roles in government. To build up good relationships with them, you not only need to meet their business needs, but you also need to support their government activities, which are very important to them. For example, there is a traditional big road show event that is held by a local banking institute. Once, after having received an invitation, a well-known American IT company decided not to participate because they thought it wasn't directly related to their business, and the company at that time was under tight cost-control pressures. The refusal was seen as a sign that they were not supporting the government activity. Furthermore, under these circumstances, the American company lost a lot of business from the other banks because the banks interpreted all of this as, "This company is experiencing financial difficulties, so it's risky to do business with."

I agree that sometimes Americans don't understand that building relationships is very important in China. It's probably for that reason that it is very difficult for them to get approval from their American headquarters for budgets on customer activities, marketing events, etc.

Another suggestion is to say that if there are issues, it is important for high-level managers to show up and be physically present; it is an important sign of sincerity and Chinese customers notice this. For example, one of our major bank customers had a technical incident that happened in one of their largest data centers. The implications were huge, and the problem needed to be resolved quickly. We sent our account manager and several of our senior engineers to go there to fix the problem; however, the bank was upset. They thought we hadn't taken it seriously enough because we didn't send our country general manager to appear on site. So our account manager had to explain to our general manager that he needed to go there in person (even though he couldn't actually do anything). It was important, however, that he show how seriously we took the problem. In the end, our general manager flew out there to meet the bank leader, and everything came out well.

I will say that American companies have made a lot of progress in management localization in China, learning that it is better to build relationships with local customers. On the other hand, however, Americans are always concerned about losing control. It's difficult to find the balance. I think a good model is that of indirect sales, where one recruits resellers to deal with customer relationships.

JIANG TAO (ROGER) SUN
STARBUCKS, TREASURY MANAGER OF GREATER CHINA REGION

My sense is that the whole idea of the importance of relationships has been a myth that Westerners have heard about doing business in China. I don't think that the role of relationships is unique to China. In fact, almost every book about management or leadership will have a section that talks about how important relationships are for both personal as well as corporate development. So I just don't buy into that.

On the other hand, I believe that this case scenario is more relevant in what it presents about dealing with government and state-owned businesses, especially where the party is the ultimate boss. Because of this, there are often gray areas in processes, procedures, policies, and regulations. When it comes to real business cases, these gray areas require official government interpretation. It really does take time to navigate through things in China to finally figure out who the key decision-makers are. Similarly, it also takes time to earn the trust from business partners so that they can support you. However, is there a fundamental cultural difference between Chinese and Americans in this? In my opinion, I doubt it. The same applies to Western cultures as well.

CHANG QING (CHRIS) LI
INTERNATIONAL BUSINESS EXECUTIVE

This case reminds me of a situation that we experienced in my company as well. The VP from our American division (I'll call him Bob) once visited China in preparation for a potential project with our Chinese division. The Chinese general manager, Guoping, invited him to a very nice traditional Chinese dinner. Bob is a "meat-and-potato" kind of guy from the Midwest. Although he was impressed with the presentation of the fancy dinner, Bob did not actually eat a lot of the food. He also did not drink much of the high-proof liquor, and as a result, Guoping took offense to this. To Guoping, not accepting the dinner was symbolic of rejecting his friendship, and there would be little chance for him to conduct any future business with Bob. Bob, on the other hand, also didn't like Guoping's management style. He thought Guoping was very rude to his employees, always shouting directions and criticisms at them. Bob was a little dubious of his Chinese counterpart's character. The dinner may have been trivial to Bob, but it was very important to Guoping, who believed that the style one shows at the dinner table reflects one's sincerity in doing business. Guoping had no idea that his management style in a hierarchical culture seemed disrespectful to Bob, but in Bob's eyes, it stood out like a thorn. Part of the problem is the Chinese like to make friends first and build a relationship before signing a business deal. They believe trust can only be earned over time, through real actions, such as the dinner that Guoping provided for Bob. Americans are just the opposite. They usually trust people from the very beginning and continue to do so unless given a reason not to. My recommendation is one of the keys to successful business with Chinese is to take time to build the relationship.

In my experience, Americans may feel that Chinese lack planning. We may set a schedule, but hardly adhere to it, and we often change things on the fly. I remember a situation when an American visitor went along with us to visit a hospital. We had set the appointment with the doctor in the morning, but the doctor did not show up and kept everyone waiting. After four hours, the doctor finally came. I remember the American was extremely unhappy, and he wanted to leave. We persuaded him to stay, and eventually, when the doctor did arrive, we got all the information we wanted. What the American did not understand was that the doctors in China, very much like the party secretaries and government officials who are mentioned in this case scenario, do not have much control over their own schedule and time. One phone call can pull them away to deal with higher-priority issues. In fact, usually, the more this happens, the more important this person is, and the more valuable it is to build a relationship with this person. He or she may hold some key information or can make the decisions to ensure your business deals are successful. So my recommendation is next time you have a chance getting to know someone like that, make sure you take the opportunity seriously.

Observations and Comments from the Authors

Anthropologists who study cultural issues often divide cultures into two camps: those that focus on the individual and those that focus on the community. North Americans, of course, are super individualists. We love to see Hollywood's heroes who take on the world. Think of every movie ever made with John Wayne, Sylvester Stallone's Rocky series, and of course, all of the Superman and Batman movies, too. When Frank Sinatra sings "I did it my way," we actually think that this is an admirable quality! It is easy to forget that many other cultures appreciate community more than individualism. Chinese culture is one of those that focuses on the needs of the community more than the needs of the individual. It only takes one stroll down Nan Jing Lu in Shanghai or one ride on the Beijing subway to appreciate the importance of community in China. Frank Sinatra's "I did it my way" is viewed as arrogance more than independence.

Jie Lo's forty years of working with people confirms the importance of community in China's professional world. This case illustrates—and Ray Brimble, A.J. Warner, Karen Boyer, and Chris Li all confirm—that important people get called away and their time is not totally their own. Notice that American individualism looks at things the opposite way. In North American culture, the more powerful you are, the less people can tell you what to do. In a community-centered society, things work the opposite way. The more powerful you are, the more people will depend on you. As Jie Lo puts it, "The higher you are, the less control you have over your own schedule." Ray Brimble advises to get used to it, because people are called away a lot. Similarly, A.J. Warner reminds us that companies have political responsibilities. Notice that North Americans do not think of companies in those terms at all.

This case also effectively illustrates the precarious situation of being asked to entertain your guests. As A.J. Warner explains, the Chinese entertainment budget is huge. Whenever Americans are in China, there is a good chance that, in the back of their minds, they are thinking, "What will I ever do to entertain these people when they visit me in the United States. There is no way I can do as much for them as they are doing for me!" The North American tendency is to put limits on expenses that can be reimbursed. There is a sense of unethical favoritism that goes with lavish entertainment expenses. In this case scenario, we are appalled at the Americans' suggestion of splitting the dinner check. As Ray Brimble says, "Run for your lives." At the same time, understand how out of balance the Chinese and American sense of entertainment truly is. Our recommendation is if you cannot reciprocate financially, there are ways to reciprocate personally. That is to say, gifts and entertainment that have personal value offset those that have greater monetary value. Weimin Chen accurately summarized that Americans build relationships to attract more business; Chinese build relationships to become friends.

The other issue that comes out in this case is that of the role of the party secretary. With private companies, this is not an issue, but in state-owned enterprises, the CEO has to be a party member, and the party secretary will be the person to confirm and communicate all of the necessary political aspects of business operations. As Jie Lo suggests, it is important not to minimize the importance of this position. Roger Sun also observed that all gray areas require government interpretation. Chinese decision-making is indeed slower. As A.J. Warner recommends, be more flexible because things take longer.

This case brings up several potential topics for further discussion. Interested readers may want to consider the talking about the following:

1. Ray Brimble hints that some of the differences expressed in this case are generational more than national. Consider some of the pros and cons of the "old school" versus the seemingly "speaker style of business development."

2. Do you find yourself sympathizing with the Americans who had to incur the expense of hosting dinner for the Chinese visitors? Or do you find yourself appalled at their lack of respect in being cheap?

3. Since Chris Li says that Bob was a "meat-and-potato" kind of guy, what approach should one take for people like him?

4. Jie Lo mentions that the American CEO who had his scheduled appointment postponed was quite put out by the whole delay. It was

also quite a cultural twist when Jie Lo told the American businessman that the party secretary had actually showed him a great sign of respect because he had begun and ended the dinner with him (even though he did need to leave in the middle of the meal). What advice do you have for people in similar situations?

5. One of the words that Jie Lo uses to describe American business professionals is naive. Based on the content of this case, what was he referring to?

6. Weimin Chen relates the story of an American IT company that decided not to participate in a local event because they felt it wasn't directly related to their business operations. Unfortunately, the refusal was seen as a lack of support of the local government activities. Furthermore, the local banks assumed that this was possibly related to financial difficulties that the IT company was going through. How do you react to this story, and what do you take away from it?

7

WǑ HUÌ SHUŌ ZHŌNGWÉN

Company: Wolcke Engineering
Focus: Internal software development for an engineering firm
Cultural Conflict: Miscommunications may increase when people use their non-native language

Introduction and Synopsis

Often, we think of English as the lingua franca in today's world. And it is true that we are able to use a lot of English in many places; however, for those who have never really studied a foreign language, it is easy to forget how difficult of a task it can be. In our own native language, we are capable of changing our meaning in such subtle ways. If we want to sound more forceful, more friendly, more convincing, or more sincere, there is usually a way to express these minute differences. What we forget is that non-native speakers seldom have that same ability. Consequently, non-native speech sounds harsh when is was intended to be soft, it sounds silly when it was intended to be serious, or it sounds simplified when the intent was to show complex details. This scenario, if it illustrates nothing else, is an excellent primer into being more understanding of what it is like for the rest of the world to have to use their non-native English language skills with us.

This case revolves around the work of Hong Shi and his role as one of the product managers at Wolcke Engineering. He leads the team of software developers, a group that often interacts with other engineers and scientists from all over the world. In this case, and among the executive comments we read, multiple examples of phrases and words cause tiny, but significant breakdowns in communication. Just think of the subtle meanings that differentiate "can, could, may, might, must, would, and will!" This case is also a good experiment in empathy, trying to feel what it is like from the Chinese perspective when trying to communicate with North Americans. There is a sense of relief when Americans like Alex Rossi come to China with an appreciation for history, geography, and the Chinese language. And there is an appreciation for how hard it would be for a Chinese person to have to stay in Dallas without the ability to drive around, or even get a taxi easily.

Case Scenario

Wolcke Engineering operates in over eighty countries, with its principal offices in Dallas, London, and Amsterdam. They focus on oil field services and have an annual revenue of $18 billion. Wolcke's 80,000 worldwide employees come from over 140 different countries. In Beijing, Hong Shi works as one of the product managers. His team focuses on software development, specifically creating programs for internal use by the company. The internal software development teams work on everything from drilling and seismic software to simulation workflows. Their objective is to build software that enables scientists to collaborate with the engineers to achieve better productivity and quality.

Hong Shi suggested that this scenario start with a brief grammar lesson comparing Mandarin and English. One wouldn't think that this is how a software development team would want to start things, but here we go. In Chinese, the verb 会 (*huì*) means "can," as in 我 会 说 中 文 (*Wǒ huì shuō zhōngwén*), or "I can speak Chinese." However, *huì* also has a wide range of other meanings. For example, it sometimes means "will," as in 他 会去北京 (*Tā huì qù Běijīng*), or "He will go to Beijing." Whenever a term in one language is translated with various options in another, there is a chance that speakers will mix up the transfer, resulting in miscommunications. This happens frequently with Hong Shi's employees, and that is why he suggested this introduction to the scenario. Native speakers of Chinese often have troubles with the nuance of words like "can, could, may, might, must, would, and will." Hong

Shi believes, "As to the actual working style, Wolcke is an international company, so the working style itself doesn't change a lot from one place to another. Our biggest challenge is more related to communication, and this is because of our non-native use of English."

Hong Shi's English is actually excellent. After graduating from the McCombs School of Business at the University of Texas at Austin, he continued to live in Texas, working for five years in Houston for another engineering firm. At this point, Hong Shi has returned to Beijing and has been working there for the past three years; however, most of the team that works with Hong Shi is composed of young graduates from local universities in Beijing, mostly from Peking University and Tsinghua University. As such, they have not had the advantage of spending extended periods of time in English-speaking countries. Generally, their English is functional, but not always polished. For example, a week prior, one of his engineers, Zhenchun Li, wrote in a memo that he "wanted an upgrade." The accounting office responded by saying, "Sorry, there isn't one." The truth is Zhenchun Li meant to say that he "needed" an upgrade. For native speakers of Chinese, the difference between "want" and "need" is a little more problematic. Recently, Hong Shi noted that another of his engineers wrote in an e-mail, "I must have a new workstation." What he really meant was it would be nice to have a new workstation. So besides saying "must" when Chinese really mean "would like to," they also say "should" when they really mean "must." And they say "want" when they really mean "can." And they say "can" when they really mean "will." You get the picture. Hong Shi adds that this is not a trivial matter. "It all adds up to miscommunications with others who do not understand where the native speakers of Chinese are coming from."

Another person who interacts with members of Hong Shi's team and who deals with communication issues is Lan Lu. Lan Lu, although born in China, has lived abroad for most of her life. Her family moved to Italy when she was thirteen, so her middle school and high school years were spent in a European system. Then Lan Lu decided to go to college in the United States, graduating in 2002 from Arizona State University with a bachelor's degree in computer science. One of Lan Lu's responsibilities is to assist employees in the preparation of their promotion files. Part of the process includes filling out a form in which the candidate is required to write a self-assessment. That is, people are supposed to talk about themselves. This self-assessment includes statements about a person's technical expertise, their abilities as leaders, their professional visibility, and their input to business strategies. The challenge is that many of the Chinese do not think of their accomplishments as accomplishments. They have been taught to be humble. Unlike independent North Americans who are used to self-promotion, the Chinese tend to tone things down a bit more. Lan Lu clarifies her challenge: "I have to push them to write two or three examples in each category. This is an international company. The same requirements for promotion exist for all of the employees, everywhere in the world." Lan Lu spends a lot of time asking people to add more examples. What many employees do not realize is senior people are going to review this file. At the initial phases, at least three to five local people need to review and support the promotion application. "Can you imagine how hard it is for us?" she asks. "Not only are we Chinese, we are engineers! Those of us who are not natural salespeople are just not as good at self-promotion." Part of Lan Lu's job is to help these employees understand that the review committees will not know them personally. Even if the local management team knows someone personally, reviewers at other levels can only base their decisions by what is actually written. Despite these challenges, it should be mentioned, that Lan Lu believes that the Chinese employees are happy with the system, even if they feel a little uncomfortable with it. There is a worldwide system for promotions. Since the company was initially created in the West, employees believe that it is a fair and balanced system.

As related to communication issues, another member of Hong Shi's software development team is Qin Mu. Qin Mu comments on his participation in video conferences, mostly with other engineers who are in the United States. "All of our non-native language issues are enhanced during these video conferences. Our problems with tense, not having plurals, nuances in meaning, etc.—they are all enhanced during video conferences." Additionally, Qin Mu notes that Chinese have a tendency to wait for others to talk first, and as a result, there is a hesitancy to share opinions. Sometimes people don't want to interrupt; other times, there are multiple conversations going on, and nobody is really listening to anybody. Still, Qin Mu would rather participate in a video conference than have to travel abroad to the home offices in Dallas. "I don't like going to Dallas because I can't drive." It is hard to get around. He complains that it's hard to get a taxi, and even if you can get a taxi from your hotel, getting one to go back to your hotel is even more difficult. As to communication, Qin Mu also thinks that it is hard to know how to handle the dinners. "Sometimes, they are really late, and I'm really hungry, but all we do is hold a wine glass and talk for a long time." Qin Mu says that it is hard to know what to say and how to keep the conversation going.

Interestingly enough, although Qin Mu does not enjoy traveling out of town, what he enjoys most is when the American representatives visit the project team in Beijing. Recently, for example, they had a visit from a product champion, Alex Rossi, who was overseeing a new product that had just been started. "From the minute that he got off the plane, he came straight to the office and started working—energetically, too." Everyone knew that he was tired after the long journey, but he still put in a full day of work. He launched into the software-tracking meetings, discussed the new version, and ended with a review of the plans and specs. By the end of the day, he had also completed a teleconference with the home office where he implemented some of the decisions that they had made during the day. Everyone was impressed. Qin Mu likes these visits. "We have good meetings and get a lot done. The lunches and dinners are with the whole team, and at the end of the day, I can go home without worrying about riding in a taxi." One more thing about Alex Rossi, Qin Mu was also impressed with the knowledge that he had about China in general. "People say that Americans don't know much about other countries, but Alex Rossi knows everything about Chinese history. He has been to a lot of places and has no problem getting around. He doesn't really know how to speak much Chinese, but could discuss Chinese history and geography in ways that even I couldn't."

Jia Bin, who has been a software engineer for six years, is another member of Hong Shi's project team who, by the way, has also traveled with Qin Mu to Dallas. He totally relates to how difficult it is to get around in Dallas. Once, he had to stay in Dallas for three months. In true Chinese diplomatic style, he says, "Fortunately, the company doesn't ask us to do that very often. I like working from nine to six from Monday to Friday where I put in my forty to fifty hours." As to the use of English,

Jia Bin likes the fact that English is the official language of the company. The company permits people to conduct meetings in the local language; however, everyone is encouraged to use English because it will help when speaking to people in other locations (e.g., Jia Bin has been working with a group of Brazilians recently). Additionally, all recognize that English is needed for promotions and other long-term opportunities. "It helps us to be more professional," he says. Jia Bin also notes that, recently, a couple of the projects were moved from the United States to Beijing. These project groups now have a number of foreigners, and as a result, everyone is speaking more English. "The people from these project groups seem to be more confident with their English. They joke more in English, and they interact more easily." This is also important because Jia Bin has seen that, in the past, the company has lost employees who were technically sound, but left because they didn't feel that their English language skills were good enough. "I hate to see good engineers who leave because of problems with English."

Hong Shi was right when he suggested that this scenario focus on communication. So next time a Chinese engineer tells you that he "wants" a computer upgrade, ask him if he "needs" it or if he "would like to have it." That verification may make a big difference.

Observations and Comments from American Experts

ARNOLD PACHTMAN (BAI WENAN)
L-3 COMMUNICATIONS GLOBAL SECURITY & ENGINEERING SOLUTIONS

Zhenchun Li wrote in a memo that he "wanted an upgrade." The accounting office responded by saying, "Sorry, there isn't one." The problem is not that nuanced terms do not exist in Chinese. In fact, it is easy to differentiate in Chinese between "want" or "like" (*xiǎngyào*), "need" (*xūyào*), "must" (*bìxū*), "should" (*yīnggāi*), "can" (*kěyǐ*), and "will" (*yào* or *huì*). The problem is, in English, the nature of the request would be clearly evident from the words alone; no context would be needed to interpret and respond to the request. In Chinese, however, the manner in which the request was made would have carried rich contextual cues to help accounting decode the request and respond in the proper way. Lacking a context to interpret and possibly approve the request, accounting told Mr. Li, "Sorry, there isn't one." This is code for, "We don't know why you are asking or why we should give you a new computer, so we will give you the standard answer to avoid a loss of face—'There isn't one.'" If, however, a manager wrote to accounting in Chinese, "It would be nice to have a new computer in our department," accounting's response would have been, "Yes, Manager Li, coming right away!"

Chinese speakers find it difficult to convey in English, using words alone, the context that is so naturally communicated in Chinese. Conversely, English speakers have problems selecting Chinese words that convey the intended meaning with English precision. In many cases, a precisely equivalent Chinese word may not exist because word choice and context are inextricably linked in Chinese. The key point is Chinese communication is 70 percent context and 30 percent literal, whereas English communication is 30 percent context and 70 percent literal. Chinese is a very terse, economical, elegant, synthetic language that builds complex concepts from simpler components—characters from radicals, words from characters, and concepts from words and context. English is a very clear, precise, analytic language that relies on grammatical constructs and syntax to a much greater degree than Chinese.

To make matters worse, all languages carve reality into a grid consisting of convenient blocks of meaning. In the case of Chinese and English, the grids do not quite line up. Therefore, you might need four English words to convey the meaning of one Chinese concept and vice versa. What all of this means is, like a swimmer venturing into unknown waters, Chinese and North Americans communicating with each other in *any* language should be mindful of all aspects of the communication—literal, contextual, cultural, verbal, and non-verbal. Never take for granted what is being said or assume that both parties have understood what was said in the manner intended.

But this case is about far more than communication; the other anecdotes all reinforce the importance of business culture. Promotions, cars, videoconferences, etc., all things taken for granted in North America, can cause serious difficulties for our Chinese colleagues, no matter how smart and technically advanced and open-minded they are. This increases the importance of being aware and tolerant of other cultures, even as North Americans attempt to establish English as the lingua franca and transplant an Anglo-centric corporate culture worldwide. Extra effort must be made to help Chinese colleagues adapt and feel comfortable with North American business culture, whether in the United States or China.

ELIZABETH FABER
DIRECTOR IN GLOBAL PROFESSIONAL SERVICES FIRM

I can relate to the scenarios at Wolcke Engineering. When living in China, I was constantly checking and rechecking my communications—in both professional and personal environments—to make sure what I meant was what was heard and vice-versa. More often than not, gaps existed due to something as fundamental as my poor Chinese speaking and comprehension skills, less-obvious cultural nuances, or something in between.

When I first began working in China, I encountered similar challenges to Lan Lu in convincing my Chinese colleagues to sell themselves. We had an opportunity to propose on a project for a client; while we had had all the right credentials to meet the project objectives, they were not precisely what the RFP requested. Had this situation occurred in the United States, my American colleagues, with complete confidence, would have marched ahead without hesitation to prepare their proposal; however, in China, I found myself working to convince my new teammates of their abilities and my confidence that we could successfully complete this engagement. They eventually agreed, helped to develop the proposal and win the work, and ultimately delivered a successful project, but it took some time upfront to help them sell themselves.

I have my own grammatical traps to add to Hong Shi's experiences with *huì*. One lesson I learned—the hard way, I might add—is the difference between "I could" in Chinese and English. When a native Chinese speaker replies to a request with *wǒ kěyǐ*, or "I could," I found it is best to interpret this answer as "no" or even "no way." Once I was tuned into this, I would even notice a distinct pause, followed by an inhalation of breath through the clenched teeth before the reply was reluctantly offered. These are all red flags that the spoken answer in Chinese and English is not the same.

Conversely, the Chinese adjective *bù cuò*, or "not bad" or "not incorrect," was considered an overwhelmingly positive reply, much more so than its English counterpart. So if a native Chinese speaker heard a native English speaker assess a situation as "not bad," he should be on alert, as "not bad" in Chinese tends to mean more good than bad, whereas English is the reverse. This difference is indicative of the humble nature of Chinese and the superlative nature of Americans.

A variety of tactics can be deployed to uncover these unintended miscommunications. First and foremost is to allow time for them to be uncovered. Rushed meetings and conference calls are fertile ground for missed connections, the magnitude of which will continue to grow if left unchecked. Plan to spend more time in conversations and, whenever possible, have these dialogues in person, in a one-on-one setting. You will learn much more in individual discussions than in group meetings, and far more in a face-to-face discussion than via a conference call. Repeat what you thought you heard your counterparts said, and ask them to confirm. Follow up with written e-mail communication to reconfirm agreements. Then, most importantly, monitor actions. Even if you did all the right things—like having a one-on-one, face-to-face meeting and reconfirming understanding verbally and via e-mail—there are no guarantees. Check in with your colleagues to make sure their actions are the same as your words. Expect them to do the same. Effective communications between multiple cultures requires time and effort, but not as much as ineffective communications!

John Hsu
Carnegie Mellon University, Master's Degree Candidate

As an American who spent a number of years working in China, my perspectives on differences in cross-cultural communications goes far beyond the fact that English words or phrases are misused or misinterpreted by Chinese associates. There are many forms of communications: verbal, written, behavioral, types of actions, cultural, etc. In the case about Wolcke Engineering, it gave a pretty good view from the perspectives of language as the basis of communications, yet significant differences also exist in the other forms of communications.

For instance, Americans tend to be very aggressive in getting what they want, but such a mentality directly conflicts with how people act inside Chinese culture, where the norm is based on how you get to know the person, how to build his or her trust, and then beginning to discussing your objectives. But, from an American perspective, such an indirect approach tends to be viewed unfavorably or as less efficient. However, to do business in China, one has to adapt and learn the way of how to appropriately build trust. In most occasions, when you are greeted with a warm welcome and a big smile from a Chinese party, it DOES NOT necessarily mean that you are actually welcomed.

Let's use another example where cultural standards affect communication. I traveled to a plant where my previous multinational corporation employer operates and learned that the CFO of that plant, who happens to also be an expatriate, dismissed local tax authorities' visits because she believed that they were implicitly asking for bribes. To make the matter worse, she disliked the governmental staff's lack of respect when they showed up at her office—first, in being late and then smoking without any intent to ask for permission. The CFO felt what she did was appropriate, given her set of standards. And I concur as well; the CFO is upholding our company's values and ethics principles. Then here comes the consequence of her actions: The plant was then regularly audited by tax authorities and was fined over 500,000 RMB in the course of the next couple years, clearly impacting the business's bottom line. Now comes the interesting question: Just imagine you are the CFO of that plant, what would you do? Through this example, it is clear that differences in cultural standards aggravate the level of communication difficulties.

Observations and Comments from Chinese Experts
WIE LI
SONY ERICSSON CHINA, CFO

This scenario is an outstanding case where non-native English speakers, who are not brought up in an English-speaking environment, have problems using the English language properly, even though their grammar is considered correct. Chinese people are taught to "remember" all their vocabulary and grammar so that they can construct sentences; however, because most of the sentences are individually separated, sometimes non-native speakers can write a correctly constructed sentence, but that doesn't mean it will be understood by native English speakers during conversations in real life. To put it another way, most Chinese people know how to construct a sentence, but they do not know how to use it properly.

Nevertheless, English is taught in a very formal way compared to the way native English speakers talk. English speakers are always surprised when someone from a non-English-speaking background uses big words, such as "irrigation." It seems strange to them that Chinese people would know a word like this, when they do not necessarily have the best English communication skills. But it's not really about the skill; it is more about the way English and non-English speakers phrase their sentences and communicate. Because of the difference, it is sometimes hard to understand one another.

From my experience, the best way to solve the problem is to create an English-speaking environment. How, you might ask? Well, there are various "tools" we can use. Good examples are English movies, TV series, songs, and books. I personally benefit a lot from the famous American TV series *Friends*. It is very relaxing and close to daily life, mainly because of the way this series seems to depict English-speaking Western life so closely. It really helped and encouraged me to speak English. I also learned a lot of helpful slang from this series.

In regards to video conferences, this can create an even more difficult situation due to the fact that you no longer have the ability to observe the person's body language and specific gestures, which can consciously and subconsciously help during the communication process; therefore, good preparation is essential.

As to suggestions, first of all, make sure that when you attend a meeting that you clearly understand the schedule, the agenda, or the minutes. Focus on details, such as who is attending the meeting, what time the meeting will start, who is giving a speech and for how long, and so on and so forth. Secondly, prepare what you are going to contribute in the meeting. You may have to consider whether you are going to give a speech as part of the fixed schedule in the meeting or if you are only going to discuss some of the issues mentioned in the meeting. You may also have to take into account the interaction and communication to other parts if there are discussion questions. Last but not least, be sure that there isn't anything that would interrupt you while you are in the meeting. One other suggestion, in this scenario, Qin Mu had a problem handling his meals when travelling. The best thing here would be to anticipate how long a meeting will last and have something to eat before the meeting.

All in all, miscommunication is a common problem between non-English-speaking people and native speakers. It even exists between native speakers from different regions and areas. To solve this problem, more training and communication are needed.

OLIVER HAN
AVARTO SERVICES, EXECUTIVE ASSISTANT TO THE VICE PRESIDENT

In my opinion, the communication problems in the scenarios are attributed to the difference between Eastern and Western cultures. In other words, they did not understand each other's culture very well. For example, first are the language issues. As everybody knows, there is usually more than one meaning for each Chinese character, and the same word can have completely different meanings, such as *huì* in the scenario. (And textbooks almost never help in telling us how to apply words to daily life, much less within cultural settings.) Therefore, non-native speakers need to practice more and try to accumulate more knowledge, which is painful. Second, we are influenced by the educational system in China. There is an old saying: "Gentleman are as tender as jade." Most Chinese people believe that it is better to be humble. From the time that we are very young, we learn that humility is a virtue. We avoid self-promotion, as expressed in the scenario, and we are more self-defacing and conservative. On the other hand, Western culture is more positive, open, and direct, and they are more willing to show what they are thinking and express themselves.

I can relate a story about this from my own experience. When I was in college, we organized an academic conference, "Unmanned Aerial Vehicle Technology Seminar." Another student and I went to the airport to pick up a foreign professor who was attending the conference. My colleague began by apologizing for her limited English: "I'm sorry that my English is not very good. I hope you will pardon me for any inconvenience it will cause." She then began to explain the history of Xi'an to this professor, all in English, which, to tell you the truth, sounded pretty good to me. During the conversation, the professor said that he knew a lot about China, and he mentioned that he could speak Chinese. Then he said some Chinese words: "hello," "thank you," and "good-bye." So she was saying that her English was bad, but she could explain the history of Xi'an in

English, and he was saying that his Chinese was good, but all he could say were a few words. It's a really good example of Eastern and Western cultural differences.

So back to how to solve the communication problem. We need more of a bridge—people like Hongshi, Jiabin, and Alex, those who can introduce the culture to others. We need more people who are willing to go abroad. At the same time, we need to invite more people to China. Even more than a bridge, we need people to share their experiences. For example, Hongshi should follow up and teach his employees about the difference between "need" and "want." Jiabin can share good examples with everyone, helping all to learn and understand. And Qinmu can share with colleagues that words like "drawer" can mean drawer, but it can also mean underwear, for example! Next, we should be bold enough to expose our problems so that we all know how to improve. After we take a few steps and make some mistakes, we need the "experts" who can identify our problems and help us improve. To summarize, we need more people to serve as our bridges, keep in touch with them, be willing to expose our mistakes, and allow them to teach us how to improve. Someone from either culture can never expect to totally understand the cultural background of another, but what we can do is keep working on it and try to integrate.

Zhen (Steve) Yang
Deloitte Consulting, Senior Consultant

I think we all relate to this one. Communicating in a foreign language is not easy. It is common to have difficulties in using foreign words precisely, especially in speaking. Chinese has limited words, and we use the same words, in different combinations or in a different context, to express different meanings. This becomes a problem when people try to translate from Chinese into English, but we do not have a large enough vocabulary to find the English with the exact meaning. Helping employees in the work environment is one way to improve this. I have also noticed that many companies nowadays rely on a standard request format. This allows people to follow a model and to select the level of urgency. This helps to avoid the misuse of words and improves efficiency.

To me, the most interesting issue in this scenario was the cultural difference between China and the West in regard to talking about one's own achievements. In China, talking about one's own achievements is regarded as showing off, which is traditionally unacceptable. In China, when a child achieves something, parents and teachers always tell the child to be humble and that he or she should set higher goals. In my own case, I still remember an experience from middle school. In my middle school, we had a weekly review for every student. One time, during the review meeting, several of my classmates talked about the mistakes they had made during the week. Since I hadn't made any mistakes, I talked about some achievement. In the end, I got the worst grade because my teacher thought that I lacked self-reflection and that I had exaggerated my achievement. It is no wonder that, under such a cultural value system, Chinese feel uncomfortable and unwilling to talk about their achievements. As to this scenario, I recommend that Wolcke Engineering have multiple methods for performance reviews: self-report, peer review, and management comments, etc. I believe this will help the company to be fair to all of the employees and to be able to retain the company's best employees.

Another issue that came out in the case is that Chinese people are friendly to foreigners, especially when the foreigner can show respect to the Chinese or speak some Chinese. For example, one of the most popular TV shows in China is where foreigners sing Chinese songs and give talk shows in Chinese on TV. In my past experience, I have found that our clients are more ready to accept ideas from foreigners when those foreigners can deliver the same content as a Chinese. I think this is part of the reason why Qin Mu appreciates Alex, because Alex knows some Chinese and shows respect to Chinese. It is always much easier to get things done in China if foreigners are willing to do that. Finally, it is sad to hear many excellent employees left Wolcke Engineering because of the language. The company should consider providing different career paths to different people. After all, the value created by employees is through what they can do rather than what they can say.

Observations and Comments from the Authors

Our experience in dealing with Chinese professionals is that they are courageous in using English. We admire their attempts to use English, despite the embarrassment or reticence that they may have. Often, their written skills are much stronger than their oral language, but we have been impressed with their command of the language and their willingness to try. And this is even true of many who have never been outside of China, as in the case of many of the engineers at Wolcke Engineering. When we conducted the interviews with the employees of Wolcke Engineering, it was clear that the use of English was thought of as a very positive aspect of their jobs. Almost everyone expressed the sentiment that it could only help them in the future by getting better at English now. Even using English with the team in Brazil was seen as a positive thing. The truth is it is much more difficult to understand foreign speech in a videoconference, and even in these situations, these professionals were willing to try. Our guess is the bandwagon to do business in China would be almost empty if Westerners were required to learn Mandarin in the same way that Chinese today are willing to learn English.

Beyond the subtleties of words such as "must, might, would, and could," the same also happens when speaking Mandarin. Elizabeth Faber gives two excellent examples in her comments. Indeed, when Chinese say *kě yǐ*, although the words mean "can," there is often more of a sentiment of, "Well, I guess you *could* if you *really* wanted to." Similarly, *bù cuò*, which literally means "not bad," has a very positive meaning in Chinese. Our recommendation is the same as hers: Check and recheck for understanding, even when you think you have it. Elizabeth concludes with another excellent observation: "Effective communication between multiple cultures requires time and effort, but not as much as ineffective communications."

Beyond vocabulary and the meaning of words, this case also presents nice evidence about how Chinese look at self-promotion. Although Wolcke Engineering has a worldwide procedure for promotions, and even though the Chinese accept the need to follow the procedure, it is still very difficult for them to engage in self-promotion. Where North Americans directly present all of the reasons why they are the "biggest and baddest," the Chinese are trained to do the opposite. Steve Yang's example where he received a lower grade in class because he talked of his achievements instead of his mistakes is a perfect illustration of this. Be humble and set higher goals. Oliver Han's story of the colleague who apologized for her limited English and then proceeded to explain the history of Xi'an to the foreign visitor was another good example of this. A portion of this comes from what John Hsu observed as the "aggressive style" with which Westerners speak.

The take-away for those of us who do not speak Mandarin is to be sympathetic when working with Chinese. Talk a little slower, user fewer slang expressions and fewer sports analogies, repeat yourself more often, write things down, use visual aids, and check and recheck to see how things are going. As mentioned in the executive comments and in the case, if you do not speak Mandarin, at least spend some time to learn about the history, geography, music, and arts so that you can engage in conversations that help "bridge" the communication gaps.

For those readers who wish to talk more about these topics with others, consider the following suggestions and questions:

1. Sit down with a Chinese colleague and discuss the nuances in the meaning of "can, could, may, might, must, would, should, and will." You will be amazed at how involved it is. Similarly, ask them about the nuances in the meaning of *huì*, and the same thing will happen from the other end.

2. Take time to assess our own use of language with foreigners. Do you tend to use phrases like, "get to first base," "hit a homerun," "strike out," "knock one out of the ballpark," etc.?

3. There are a few references in the case about engineers who have good technical skills but limited English language skills. It seems a shame to lose good engineers because of foreign language proficiency. Any suggestions about what to do about this?

4. Can you think of instances where foreigners give the impression of being angry, bored, super excited, or overly happy. Look back and think about how some of this may be a misrepresentation of their emotions, based on limitations in native-like proficiency in English.

5. What advice do you have for Lan Lu, who helps assist the employees as they prepare their promotion file? On the other hand, what advice do you have for those who read the promotion files?

6. Arnold Pachtman observes that Chinese communication is 70 percent context and 30 percent literal, whereas English communication is 30 percent context and 70 percent literal. He illustrates this by saying that Chinese build complex concepts from simpler components—

characters from radicals, words from characters, and concepts from words and context. English, he claims, is a more precise, analytic language that relies on grammatical constructs and syntax to a much greater degree than Chinese. What might he be referring to with these statements?

8

CARPE DIEM

Company: QingWen Software
Focus: Software development projects for American and Chinese clients
Cultural Conflict: There is a sense that Chinese focus on speed, while Americans focus on quality. But is this really true?

Introduction and Synopsis

At first blush, this is a case about American efficiency and Chinese disregard for quality in the development of software. But as you look deeper, you see that many of the actions of Chinese firms and employees are driven by the significant difference between the rate of growth of the Chinese and American economies. In China, growth is explosive, and there is a great sense of urgency. Firms and employees feel the need to "seize the day" and move as quickly as possible. Everyone in China knows that double-digit growth cannot last forever, and they want to make sure that they get as much as they can before things slow down.

In America, growth is much slower, systems are more developed, and there is a greater concern about "predictability." This may seem "superior" to Americans, until one remembers how things were during the "go-go" years of the 1990s.

Another contextual issue is China's recent history of complete state control over every aspect of every Chinese citizen's life. Today's generation is the first to have complete freedom to do what they want, work where they want, and to make as much money as possible. As a result, the current generation and their parents have a tremendous need to "catch up" financially for all of the years where their earning potential was limited.

The net-net of this case is one cannot understand what is going on in China if one does not understand China's recent political, cultural, and historical past. It is also important for one to not forget America's recent go-go years history when one assesses what is going on in China during this period of rapid growth.

In this case, although Yang Wang is Chinese, he first got experience in the software development industry while living in Canada. Now he is back in China and finds himself going through a reverse culture shock, adapting back into a more Chinese way of doing things.

Case Scenario

Academic scholars tell us that there are literary motifs, e.g., *momento mori*, or "Remember you are human," and *ubi sunt*, or "Where are they?". One of the most famous literary motifs is *carpe diem*, or "Seize the day." The famous *carpe diem* may not apply more anywhere in the world than it does in Shanghai. A look at the Pudong skyline along the Huangpu River exudes a sense of *carpe diem*, showing off the former fishing village as China's most vibrant financial and commercial center of the modern world. Of course, Shanghai is unique, but in some ways, every aspect of business in China has this underlying feel of *carpe diem*. There is an interesting blend of traditional Chinese long-term perspective and the new China now! No one exemplifies this more than Yang Wang, chairman and CEO of QingWen Software. QingWen Software provides software development outsourcing for customers all over the world. In fact, even though they are based in Shanghai, over 80 percent of his clients are North Americans.

In 2005, Yang Wang ran a small software development company in Vancouver, Canada. An American company acquired them in 2007, so he returned to his native China and started QingWen Software. If you ask him about the cultural issues related to his business, he is quick to observe that, for him, many of the cultural issues relate to his work with local Chinese more than the Americans. "Since I first started a business in Canada, I got used to the Western cultural issues the first time around." By the time he started his current company in Shanghai, he had already become accustomed to the business side of things. "For example," he says, "in Western cultures, people are more focused on quality. Here in China, people are more focused on speed." In the United States, Yang Wang would have to create more demos and pilot projects. It took a little longer to get things started, but U.S. companies were more willing to take the time to see what the finished product would look like. Basically, Yang Wang believes that Americans like to do things step by step. They want to start with a statement of the project, followed by references from previous customers. Then they want price quotes, a demo phase, a pilot project, and finally, the building stage, which, of course, will have multiple checkpoints along the way. "By comparison, in China, they just want to know how fast we can get the software developed. The step-by-step approach is time-consuming, and that is why many Chinese don't want to do it." Strangely enough, Yang Wang confesses that he prefers American clients.

While in Canada, Yang Wang also gained experience in doing cold calling. He made thousands of calls. At first, it was hard for him because cold calling not only means that you have to talk to people who you do not know, but it also means that you have to tell them that you are the best and the greatest. That style takes some getting used to when you are Chinese. In China, Yang Wang has hired a sales manager who is also doing cold calling in China. There are some differences, however. For example, Yang Wang laughs that many Western people associate the Internet with adult entertainment and sexual solicitations. "People misunderstood the idea of what it means to develop websites. We'd have to tell them that we weren't selling adult entertainment. It's weird because nobody in China thinks that we're into adult entertainment." Still, cold calling has limited results, but it is a normal procedure for software development companies.

Another thing that Yang Wang got used to in Western culture was the way people pay for services. "Here in China, clients typically delay payments more, so we have to push to get the client to pay." He noticed that a credit history is more important in the United States. Companies do not want to have a reputation for not paying, so he seldom had to pressure people to pay. Usually, they would just follow the agreed-upon dates. That is not his experience in China. For example, two years ago, Yang Wang started a sixty-month project with a client in the southern part of China. In the contract, the company was required to pay a monthly sum for research and development. When it came time to collect, after the first month, they said, "Sorry, our cash flow this month is low." Yang Wang figured that would be all right because he knew this was going to be a large, long project. After six months of the same response, and after lots of negotiating, they finally started their payments. "Sometimes these kind of things can go on for years." On the other hand, when Yang Wang was in Vancouver, he once made the mistake of pushing for payment with a client he had been working for. The project was almost completed, and he figured it would be a good time to collect. "In the end, they didn't give us a good recommendation, and I know that the quality of our actual work was excellent. I think they didn't like being pushed for a payment." Yang Wang now knows he shouldn't have pushed for that payment. He's sure it was perceived as a lack of trust.

Training is another area where Yang Wang has tried to make adjustments on his return to China. "In the West, training is encouraged, and individuals are willing to do so. Employees like to understand the big picture beyond just their individual duties. Here in China, employers sometimes think of training as a risky expense. They are afraid that the newly trained employee will take those new skills and go to a different company." Where the Americans are more concerned about losing confidential information (hence the disclosure clauses), Chinese are more concerned about losing skilled workers to the competition. At QingWen Software, Yang Wang tries to encourage his employees to better their skills and training. To help with the "big picture," he has created a program called "open explorer." New employees are encouraged to visit any other department or employee and ask any question they want about how things are run. He had seen that in Vancouver and was trying to implement that same thing in his new Shanghai office. "It is going slower here, but some like it and are getting used to it," he confesses.

QingWen Software has grown well. Yang Wang currently has thirty employees in the Shanghai office. He recently hired a new English translator, and he was in the process of interviewing promising candidates for a new database administrator as well as a new software architect. Everyone in the office is Chinese, and all have university degrees from schools in China. His system administrator worked in Finland for six years, but other than that, none have ever worked outside of China. "Since 80 percent of our work is with Americans, we have to communicate a lot with people in English. I've been impressed with our employees' ability to talk to people in English. A lot of our contact is via e-mail, and we can understand the technical engineers just fine." However, sometimes it is more difficult to understand the CEOs because the conversations are less technical and filled with more idioms.

Things are going well for QingWen Software; the demand for work in software development outsourcing, software distribution outsourcing, and business process outsourcing continues to grow, both among American and Chinese clients. Finally, and this has nothing to do with the actual company but everything to do with *carpe diem*, if you ever visit with Yang Wang, be sure to stop by the restaurant that is just across the street from his office. It definitely has the best 水煮鱼 (*shuǐ zhǔ yú*) in town!

Observations and Comments from American Experts
RAY BRIMBLE
LYNXS GROUP, PRESIDENT AND CEO

The Zeitgeist of today's Shanghai business world, described as "*carpe diem*," can also be described as simply "opportunistic." These attitudes may be the result of a combination of increased business opportunities, combined with a vague sense that "this may all go away someday, so we have to make it while we can." Americans have the luxury of incrementalism. Incrementalism is the result of years of trial and error resulting in "best practice." But today's China may be about "speed to market" rather than best-practice sustainability.

As Chinese try to deal with the demands of a rapidly expanding economy, as well as an ever-expanding opportunity universe, it all must look a little bit like Disneyland to the college-educated entrepreneurs and staff of this software company. So details like business plans, cold calling, and paying bills on time may not seem like the necessities they are in the West. But the boom times will someday change to a more challenging business environment. The skills brought to China by Yang Wang, honed in on the less-opportunistic environment of Canada, where I assume he lived and worked during the less booming times there, will be invaluable when a future economic situation will separate the "wheat from the chaff." This separation often depends on companies, and individuals, adopting more precise, competitive, and customer-friendly approaches, which have been adopted in the West out of the necessities of past downturns and everyday stiff competition.

TIM HOLLINGSHEAD
THE HOLLINGSHEAD GROUP, PRESIDENT AND CEO

In reviewing the case presented involving Yang Wang, my overall impression is empathy because I identify with some of the challenges he faces in his business repatriation. Overall, the Chinese belong to a culture that has less experience in creatively solving business issues. They are true to their heritage in terms of being humble and willing servants rather than experienced in "out-of-the-box" business solutions.

My experience in working in China revolves around the distribution and future manufacturing of our own branded product. In every one of our discussions with investors and distributors, they have never asked us to address the issue of quality. Instead, the focus has been all about how fast a factory could be assembled and how fast the product could be produced. Our Chinese counterparts were anxious to build the factory and produce the product without much thought to distribution. We manufacture dietary supplements in a liquid form. Interestingly enough, Chinese have less concern for the taste of the product as they have for how it feels in their mouth. Was it cold or hot? Was it smooth or rough? Was it soft or hard? Flavor was less important. Here in the West, it is all about the flavor and much less about consistency. At the same time, the Chinese seem to understand, from a cultural point of view, the importance of natural dietary supplements. Just step into a Chinese pharmacy and look into the wooden drawers typically found along the wall. You will find herbs, spices, and other most curious and disgusting elements used in the art of healing. While on a recent trip, one of our travel companions from the United States became ill. I was able to easily find a stethoscope at a local pharmacy. However, when we went to the hospital located just across the street from our hotel, the only doctor available was one trained in Chinese medicine and acupuncture. Being a physician, I was able to describe the type of Western medication we were seeking. After thumbing through a Chinese/English dictionary of medical terms and medicines, I found what we were looking for. Our most-accommodating Chinese doctor also prescribed a Chinese herbal remedy. He had prescribed some foul-smelling, black, tar-like liquid made from the digestive tract of a marine animal. The pharmacy attendant tried to convince us that the remedy had a most-appealing feel in the mouth; however, the smell and taste were most disagreeable. Anyway, back to our product—in China, it has passed the "mouth feel" test. There was no mention of the taste.

As related to Yang Wang's situation, I have also run into the same obstacles regarding payment in China. It seems that the Chinese want to meet and sign contracts, but when the issue of payment or even a down payment arises, the response is always the same. They want to sell the product first and then pay when they feel it has sold enough. They are much less experienced in the area of deposits and "buy-in." In the West, we use these techniques to mitigate risk and ensure cooperation from both sides. My experience is that this in not so in China. My recommendation is you need to prepare your Chinese counterpart. Encourage them through a sort of proactive *carpe diem*. Let them come to terms and allow them the space to perform prior to signing contracts. Use that mark of performance as their opportunity to "seize the day."

JEFF BOCK
MICROCONTROLLER SOLUTIONS GROUP, GLOBAL MARKETING MANAGER

Two of Yang Wang's assertions affect my work in China every day: tradeoffs of speed versus quality and the ability of Chinese team members to communicate subtlety in English. I find these two issues to be intimately related to each other, and without careful management, they can definitely make projects unsuccessful. How do communication issues and a focus on finishing quickly cause projects to fail? First, due to "face" concerns, Chinese team members may be unwilling to raise quality issues or highlight problems to the broader team. They may be concerned about protecting their own reputation or do not want to be perceived as damaging the reputation of other team members. Second, the push to do things quickly is definitely quite strong. Hence, people may make mistakes of omission due to trying to do things too quickly. Third, business and marketing issues are often much more subtle than technical discussions and require a deeper understanding of the context. Many people you might hire in China may have limited experience dealing with global teams and communicating across cultures. Hence, complicated multinational projects are ripe for opportunities to focus on speed versus quality and to make errors due to lack of understanding. Finally, the experience and perspective of the average Chinese employee is still less than the average employee in my American team, so the employee's quality screen and attention to detail may not be as high. So how does a manager help coach team members to avoid these pitfalls?

- *Feed-Forward*: Anticipate the issues that could cause the biggest problems on the project, then step through the likely scenarios for those issues with team members ahead of time. Make sure to clearly state goals for success and paint a *very* clear picture of what success looks like. Have the team leaders articulate what success means in written form to make certain they understand, and review regularly with key team stakeholders.

- *Hands-on Management*: I have found that the best way to help the team be successful is to be more hands-on with critical projects than I tend to be in America. Over time, this may not be necessary, but while our team is still growing and learning, I've found it necessary and indispensable to make certain that everyone around the world understands each other, is aware of key project risks and milestones, and is willing to discuss issues with each other openly.

- *One-on-Ones*: Pull key team members aside every other week or so and discuss the project with them. Ask team members about critical project milestones, ask what they are concerned about, ask what they think is going well…JUST ASK. I have found one-on-one conversations with my Chinese team members absolutely essential to make certain that all issues are being raised, and if I determine all team members do not understand something, I raise it personally to avoid any face issues for team members.

It is only through direct and regular management involvement to push for quality and to bridge communication that the day you seize can be a guaranteed success!

Observations and Comments from Chinese Experts

Quan (Michael) Zheng

Beijing BizTravel International Travel Service Company, Partner

After finishing reading this case, I was touched by it in many ways. In today's China, particularly in more developed coastal areas, such as

Shanghai, Chinese become more and more impatient, are eager for quick success and immediate gain, and lack long-term view for the enterprise and individual career development.

This thirty-year period of time, after China implemented economic reform and an open-door foreign policy, China's speed of development has been phenomenal, and the change has been tremendous. Chinese people are eager to seize any opportunity so they can improve their quality of life. The craving for speed has caused the executives to neglect product quality and brand-building, while, for individuals, their drive for higher salary prevents them from planning their career for the long run. The company hopes to maximize profits by speed to market; the employee hopes for promotion and higher salary by frequently switching jobs. Thus, companies ignore the importance of product quality and market research, and they completely avoid investment in training due to high employee turnover.

In my opinion, the reason all these scenarios happen is due to the lack of an established credit system for both the company and the individual. Because of a deficient credit system, neither the company nor the employee takes responsibility for the company and society. The company does not take credit risk into consideration when violating a contract. Thus, the contract loses its binding force. Individuals break employment contracts and switch to higher-paying jobs at will.

To solve these problems, there is a pressing need to build a comprehensive credit system for both the individual and the company. Only with a fully established credit system will the increased cost of losing credibility force the company and the individual to make decisions with a long-term view and to value its own credibility. Only then will the company pay more attention to its own reputation in the business world, while pursuing profit. Only then will the company feel it is natural to comply with the binding force of a contract. And only then will it make sense for a company to emphasize employee training and development. At the same time, the individual will then pay attention to the company's long-term development and not just their own momentary personal gain.

In China's travel industry, the issues raised in the case are very typical, particularly for a travel agency that provides domestic travel services. It is very common for the group travel agency to postpone payment to the downstream local reception travel agency. Most travel agencies are not willing to develop their own programs, so they simply copy other travel agencies' routes and programs. A common sales practice is to use a lower price to attract customers and to make up the profit through shopping kickbacks or by increasing more items that are not covered in the package—and completely ignore customer service. Before new employees start, there is no training. This practice has fundamentally tarnished the image of the company, and the domestic tourist industry in general. High turnover of tour guides is rampant. In light of the above situation, our company gave up on the domestic travel business years ago.

WEIMIN CHEN
GREATER CHINA HQ, CHANNEL OPERATIONS MANAGER

Indeed, as mentioned in this case, a difference in payment does exist in our daily work. For example, Chinese customers know they have power, as it relates to payment, and sometimes, they use this power to negotiate deals. The terms of payment are different for every contract and with different customers, and they are getting more and more complicated as competition becomes more intensive. For example, a customer might like to pay a 5 percent down payment, and then another 40 percent on delivery, and 40 percent after machine testing is completed, and the final 15 percent after twelve months. So in order to show revenues, especially at the end of a quarter or at the end of a year, the main job of the sales department is to push customers to sign related documents and to collect money from customers in a timely manner. In fact, I remember one time when sales got a really large check from an important account just two hours before the end of the quarter final cut-off time! To avoid some of these payment issues, what I've seen is a lot of the American companies preferring to use an indirect sales model. The American companies recruit other local companies who function as distributors and resellers to the end-users. Of course, the big advantage of the indirect sales model is that the American companies don't need to worry about signing contracts or collecting payments from end-users. The distributors and resellers have to pay 100 percent payment on delivery, and then they handle all of the contracts and payments with the customers. Of course, they will get a discount by doing this, but more and more American companies are using an indirect sales model in China. It's straightforward and easy to operate.

Also, as mentioned in this case, another big pressure for foreign companies that are doing business in China is that of the price. Chinese customers are more focused on price than they are on quality. Most of the big purchases in China are based on an open bid. And when it comes to open bid, price is always the first priority. If a company can't be competitive with the price, even if the product is of a high quality, it will still be knocked off from the bid because of the price. For example, a buyer may choose three vendors who offer a good price, and then they'll compare their products. What we often hear from our customers is, "Sorry, we know that your product is good, but we have a budget, and your price is too high."

As to training, just as was mentioned in this case, we worry about losing trained workers to others. Training is a big concern for companies in China, especially the middle- to small-sized companies. I think this is partially because the Chinese economy is booming and there are a lot of job opportunities in the market. The turnover rate is higher than in most of the areas of the world. It's relatively easy for skilled people to find better opportunities with better pay. For example, one of my friends is running a small software company in Beijing. He told me that most of the new graduates he hired would work in his company for maybe one or two years to get some experience and training, but then they would leave for better opportunities. In fact, in this instance, he didn't want to invest more in employee training because he knew that the more training they got, the sooner they would leave. As a small company, he couldn't offer what the big companies could in terms of opportunities and packages. Even in my company, which is a big company, the turnover rate is still very high. The average working duration of an employee is about two to three years. My company tries to keep employees by providing them with stock options for five years and with the limitation that they can only sell 20 percent per year.

Finally, I wanted to mention how interesting it is to see how Americans and Chinese vendors work on projects. I am currently involved in two projects—a global-level outsourcing project to an American vendor and a local project that involves a Chinese vendor. As soon as the project started, the American vendor provided us with a detailed project timeline, complete with accomplishment dates. When the timeline is approved, it's firm. Then everyone will follow the deadline of each stage. Regular meetings are arranged to review the status of the project. Every one knows where they are and where to go, and everything is on track. On the other hand, the Chinese vendor has a more flexible timeline. The meetings seem more like open discussions. No one knows exactly what the topics are going to be until the meeting starts. There is no firm timeline for the project. The vendor usually tells us something like, "We will send you the proposal in about two weeks." And no one is surprised if they send the proposal in three weeks. What we have is a general sense that the project will be completed sometime next quarter. Of course, it would be better to set up detailed criteria and a timeline and then ask the vendor to follow up.

JULIA GUO HUIMIN
CHINDEX MEDICAL LTD., OPERATION DIRECTOR

Yang Wang's experiences reminded me of one of my former colleagues who had a very similar experience. He was a supervisor of an IT department in a Chinese bank before he went abroad. When he went to Canada, he was a software programmer in our company. Then he was promoted to be the software development manager, and he was sent back to China as a software development manager last year. However, because of the different working habits and because of some family reasons, he went back to Canada one year later. We often talked about these differences when he was in China, and it was impossible for him to change back. He preferred the North American working style.

My colleague also complained a lot about clients who only looked for speed instead of quality. They did not plan ahead, and they did not care about making models. They wanted everything to be fast, and "enough for tomorrow" is fine. All of the requests are for "tomorrow," and quality was something to worry about in the future, and the clients thought that you could always help fix it later. This problem exists in all areas in China, and I think the reasons are, first, society is developing fast, and if we do it after everything is ready, even the pilot study may not meet the demands anymore; secondly, China's economy developed slowly in the previous thirty years, and people did not need to plan. Planning was something for the government and the leaders; we only needed to "listen" and listen to the "arrangement." This habit exists everywhere today. If your clients are not good at planning, they will often find something due tomorrow, and they will need you to do it today. In that case, completing the task is more important than good quality, and in this environment, foreign companies need to teach clients how to plan ahead, for example, trying to explain your working procedure and the needs of delivery before signing the contract, what the benefits to them are, and then you will need to visit them regularly and check the information and work progress you need from the clients. By doing this, things might improve, but it won't completely resolve everything.

In China, doing business depends on relationships or references from friends and clients, and it is hard to do business by unexpectedly soliciting potential clients. Because there is no evidence-based credit system in the whole country, people are very alert, and it takes a long time to establish trust, and they need someone they both trust. Trust is based on their previous experience, human sense, and intermediaries. Even when business is done through relationships or by references from friends, payment is always a big problem. It is a macro-sized problem, and without credit system constraints, every company is owed by its customers, and they have to default their suppliers to relieve pressures on cash flow. Therefore, foreign companies have to maximize down payments when they sign a contract, and they bundle the rest of the payments with post services.

In China, only the famous international companies have great training and employee development programs. Beyond those, not to mention the domestic companies, not even the strongest five hundred foreign companies have good training or development programs. All the companies that I have worked for are among the strongest five hundred, and I received great training in my first company. I signed a three-year contract to ensure that I would stay in the company after training. After the contract expired, a second company came to my first company and "dug" people out by offering them a higher salary. The companies that care about training basically prepare human resources for other companies. Because most of these foreign companies in China are sale-oriented companies, the human resources are primary in production and processing areas, which all depend on the employees' experiences and customer resources. They do not rely on "confidential" information very much. In cases like this, we can learn from the practices of my first American employer. This company consistently relied on training, including course training and job training, and they focused on consistent human resource reserves and promotions to ensure that their business would not be affected by certain employees. But a practice such as this requires a lot of financial support and an established human resource system, which is not appropriate for companies of all sizes.

Observations and Comments from the Authors

As mentioned in the introduction, this case is not as much about speed versus quality as it is about being opportunistic during the development phase; however, things will slow down at some point, and then best-practice sustainability will follow. In the meantime, beyond the economic issues, there are a number of cultural ones that stand out in this case, too. It is always helpful to remind ourselves that cultural issues are not simply some quirky, random tendency. There is a good reason why people do the things they do. For example, in a society that has less of a developed credit system, it only becomes more important to depend on good relationships with the people you do business with. Similarly, cold calling becomes even more difficult in a society that does less business with total strangers. North Americans would also be reticent about training employees if a large portion of them would be leaving for the competitor within a short amount of time. If Americans were more concerned with saving face, they would also find it more difficult to report on problems with quality, especially if it makes a colleague of yours look bad.

As to training, Jeff Bock provides three excellent suggestions when working with Chinese: feed-forward, hands-on management, and one-on-one interactions. As he says, just ask! Keep the lines of communication open. From the financial side, Weimin Chen suggests that an indirect sales model will help in securing payments.

One of the issues that comes up time and time again is the lack of employee loyalty in China. Employers do not want to train employees because they fear that the investment will be wasted when the employees leave for other firms. On the surface, this seems to be a uniquely Chinese phenomenon, until you think back to how things were in the United States during the Internet boom. Back then, business plans were written on cocktail napkins, no one had time for training in the race to be "first to market," software companies shipped products with thousands of known bugs, and firms that were marginally profitable "went public" so that their employees and investors could cash in before "the party stopped." Employee loyalty was entirely based on the expected value of the firm's stock. If it looked like the firm was not going to have explosive growth, American employees jumped ship without a second thought. We all know what happened when the Internet bubble burst at the beginning of the 21st century.

Many of the topics raised in the executive comments are worthy of further discussion. For those who wish to do so, here are a few potential questions for discussion:

1. What is your opinion of Ray Brimble's observation that the skills Yang Wang brought with him from Canada will serve him well in the coming years as China moves from an opportunistic to an incremental phase?

2. Think of practical applications to Jeff Bock's recommendations related to feed-forward, hands-on management, and one-on-one. How do issues of "face" relate to a person's unwillingness to raise issues of quality?

3. Michael Zheng mentions that, for both the customer and the company, the lack of an established credit system is one of the challenges in resolving the problem of payment. What suggestions can you make to help both "take responsibility" for payment?

4. Discuss the advantages and disadvantages of following Weimin Chen's suggestion that a company adopt an indirect sales model to resolve payment issues.

5. What recommendations can you think of to address the issue of training, knowing that the turnover rate of employees is extremely high? Discuss how the issues of training and quality are related.

6. Yang Wang talked of his experience doing cold calling. At the same time, Julia Guo Huimin made some observations about how business in China depends on relationships and references from friends and clients. Are both viable?

LIST OF CONTRIBUTORS

American Contributors

Robert Berki is a lead systems engineer for a major lighting company. Robert has been involved in product validation and the transfer of manufacturing technology and quality systems to China for the past seven years. He has over twenty years of experience in the lighting industry, including positions in product design, halogen cycle research, analytical methods development, quality systems, Six Sigma, and product safety. Robert holds an MS degree in chemistry from Cleveland State University.

Jeff Bock (包杰夫 - Bao Jie Fu) is global marketing manager within the Microcontroller Solutions Group of Freescale Semiconductor. Jeff has general responsibility for driving global product launch and promotion strategies for all eight-, sixteen-, and thirty-two-bit microcontrollers targeted at consumer and industrial spaces. He leads the efforts of a team of marketing personnel from around the world, with specific focus on penetrating emerging markets for embedded design, such as China, India, and Eastern Europe. He has over twelve years of experience within the semiconductor industry, including positions in wafer manufacturing, product engineering, and product marketing. Jeff holds an MBA from the University of Texas at Austin and a BS in chemical engineering from the University of Wisconsin at Madison. He is currently based in Shanghai, China, and can be contacted at jmbock@gmail.com.

Karen Boyer (红叶) spent seven years living and working in Asia. Her interest in Asia started out with a simple conversation with a Chinese friend who found Karen's ideas on China to be hilariously far from reality.

At her friend's suggestion, she left the United States to see the world. After spending two years in Japan and five years in China, Karen returned to the United States with a new perspective on Asian cultures that she is eager to share. While in China, she embraced the Chinese culture and learned to speak conversational Mandarin. Karen currently works in the marketing department of Goodwill Industries of Central Texas. She also does consulting on how to adjust to new cultures for families moving abroad. She can be reached at karenmarieboyer@yahoo.com.

Raymond J. Brimble is founder of the Lynxs Group of Companies, international developers of air cargo facilities with operations in North America, Europe, and Asia. In 2007, Lynxs was partially acquired by General Electric Commercial Aviation Services (GECAS), a wholly owned division of General Electric Corporation and the world's largest lessor of aircraft. Before forming Lynxs, Mr. Brimble owned several international trade–related companies, including Jetfill International and Loosbrock World Trade and Supply Company and manufactured and distributed products in more than fifty countries worldwide. Mr. Brimble taught international business at the University of Texas at Austin for three years, was an associate director of the Center for International Business Education and Research at the University of Texas at Austin McCombs School of Business, and is the author/editor of two books on international trade–related subjects.

Elizabeth Faber (范丽莎) is an American who has worked and lived in Asia Pacific for the last six years. After working in a Big Four consulting practice in the United States for ten years, she moved with the firm to Shanghai to advise MNCs that require strategic, operational, and implementation assistance as they enter or expand into China. She is currently a director in Singapore focused on the Southeast Asia market. Ms. Faber has an MBA from Southern Methodist University in Dallas and a BS from the University of North Carolina at Chapel Hill.

Andy Ferguson is general manager of South Mountain China Tours. An American business executive who has variously worked, traveled, or lived in China since 1978, he speaks Chinese fluently and does consulting work for U.S. companies wanting to buy, sell, or manufacture there. He is now semi-retired and spends time planning and leading specialized

Chinese cultural tours. He is the author of *Zen's Chinese Heritage: The Masters and their Teachings*. He can be reached at andyf@sonic.net.

Timothy S. Hollingshead, DPM, is a board-certified surgeon specializing in the treatment of injuries and ailments affecting the foot, ankle, and lower leg. He is a professor of biology, anatomy, and physiology at Southern Utah University and Dixie State College. He is a national lecturer and author, medical practice consultant, and consultant to the nutraceutical industry. He is a successful businessman, president, and CEO of the Hollingshead Group. Dr. Hollingshead is also fluent in Spanish and Portuguese.

David Hollingsworth has worked in semiconductor manufacturing for twenty-seven years. He has a chemical engineering degree from the University of Texas. Mr. Hollingsworth is currently the business manager for Freescale's final manufacturing operation, with facilities in Kuala Lampur, Malaysia, and Tianjin, China.

John Hsu (徐慶強) is an international business executive with over nine years of experience in business consulting, information systems management, and product management. He worked for five years as a regional IT executive based in Beijing and Shanghai, where he was a part of global 500 MNC's Asia management team responsible for tripling the firm's growth in just three years and was later promoted to manage the firm's North America IT operations in the United States. John is fluent in English and Chinese. He is currently pursuing a master's degree from Carnegie Mellon University, and he holds a BS in electrical engineering and computer science from the University of California, Berkeley. He may be contacted at jqhsu@engineeralum.berkeley.edu.

Dave Landis (蓝大卫) has worked in the Silicon Valley since 1990 in the semiconductor industry and has enjoyed the presence of a strong Chinese community. He has learned to speak elementary Chinese because of family, coworkers, and his interest in Tai Chi. His goal is to become proficient in the language. Dave is also the creator of the blog mychinaconnection.com.

Magnus & MingXing Larsen is a husband-and-wife creative team who have, together, developed a new web destination! Magnus and MingXing run their websites www.MandMx.com and www.ChineseComicsOnline.

com, which contain unique stories about China, along with the first-ever bilingual English/Chinese comic strip. The comics have been featured on a number of popular China sites, including Chinasmack.com, Sinosplice.com, and LostLaowai.com and have the potential of reaching millions and millions more in both languages! Magnus is an American cartoonist from western Massachusetts with five-plus years of experience living and working in China. MingXing is a local Shanghainese from Shanghai PRC with over four years overseas work and life experience. They also feature their son on *Study Chinese with Ryan* (睿恩学中文) videos, which are a runaway hit on Youku and Youtube. If you are curious about the Shanghai dialect, they also offer a Shanghainese (上海话) podcast. They both love China as well as the cross-cultural life that they've chosen.

Arnold Pachtman (白文安) is an international business executive and consultant with over seventeen years of experience in technology marketing, business management, and Six Sigma. He worked for three years as a researcher in Shanghai, where he was the first foreigner issued a Chinese Academy of Sciences work permit, and four years as a project engineer at E&C Engineering Corporation in Taipei, where he was the first foreign employee. He also spent five years traveling in Latin America. Dr. Pachtman is fluent in English, Chinese, Spanish, and Portuguese and has over a hundred publications and reports to his credit. He holds an MBA with honors from the University of Texas at Austin and a PhD in engineering from MIT. He currently works with L-3 Communications Global Security & Engineering Solutions. He may be contacted at pachtman@alum.mit.edu.

James (Jim) Satloff is an experienced chief executive and senior manager with a twenty-five-year track record of global leadership in financial services and technology. He has served as CEO and president of multiple broker-dealers and is a leader in the use of technology in financial services and media. He is currently venture partner at Yellowstone Capital and serves as the U.S. representative of the China-based private equity and advisory services firm. His responsibilities include leveraging an extensive personal network of financial market participants in order to facilitate the identification and acquisition of U.S. market partners for firm clients. The capital market services client set consists of high-quality, China-based companies, both pre-public as well as public. The advisory services client set consists primarily of U.S.-based companies with operations or acquisition targets in China. James can be reached at james@satloff.com.

Amber Scorah spent six years learning Mandarin Chinese and experiencing Chinese culture firsthand in Taiwan and Mainland China. Amber previously hosted a podcast about China and Chinese culture called *Dear Amber* that was rated in iTunes as one the top 10 podcasts of 2008. She now resides in New York City, just up the street from Chinatown, and continues her Chinese journey as host of a podcast called *Amber's Chinese Buffet*, which can also be found on iTunes.

A.J. Warner (华安杰) established Touchdown! into one of China's leading educational consulting companies since starting the firm back in 2005. A.J. focuses primarily on coaching clients to enter top U.S. business programs. After first arriving in China, he performed consulting projects for six of China's leading IT outsourcing companies. He was invited to speak at numerous outsourcing industry events and consulted to the Beijing Municipal Government. He also worked with Chinese start-up companies, helping them meet with leading VC firms in Beijing and Silicon Valley to secure investments. Prior to moving to Beijing, A.J. worked for Deloitte Consulting in Dallas as a manager. He holds an MBA from the University of Texas, where he received a full scholarship and an undergraduate degree from the University of Illinois Urbana-Champaign. He is the Texas MBA Beijing Alumni Chapter president. He may be contacted at ajwarner@touchdown.org.cn.

Sandor Weiss (万若山) has worked on numerous international transactions as an international tax advisor, mergers and acquisitions specialist, and project finance specialist over the course of his career, which began in 1981. Mr. Weiss is a U.S. CPA by training and has worked with some of the largest and most respected financial services companies in the world. Living and working in the United States, Singapore, Malaysia, Indonesia, the United Kingdom, and Greater China has given Mr. Weiss a wide variety of international business and transactional experience. He may be contacted at sandor.weiss@milnerweiss.com.

Chinese Contributors

Weimin Chen is currently working in an American IT company, Greater China HQ, located in Beijing. She started her career by working in a government institute of China. This period of working experience gave her a deep understanding of Chinese government structure and operation. She also has work experience in a global American company, working in the Canadian branch in Toronto after she completed an MBA program at the University of Ottawa.

Shou Zheng (Jeffrey) Cheng is currently working at Russell Reynolds Associates, a global executive search firm. Based in Shanghai, he focuses on chief executives, board of directors, financial officers, and functional corporate and business unit officers assignments for international clients. Before returning to China, Jeffrey was working for Russell Reynolds Associates in both the Houston and Toronto offices. Prior to RRA, he held an operations management position at CME Mercantile Group, Canada. Prior to that, he worked at China Grain Reserves Corporation, in the Shanghai Branch. Jeffrey is a member of the Association of Chartered Accountants (ACCA, UK) and the Chinese American Petroleum Association. Jeffrey received his MBA from the University of Texas at Austin and a BM degree in Finance and Accounting from the University of Shanghai for Science and Technology. He can be contacted at Jeffrey. Cheng@russellreynolds.com.

Julia Guo Huimin (郭慧敏) Chindex Medical Ltd., Operation Director.

Oliver Han (韩鹏) currently serves as executive assistant to the vice president of Arvato Services (China), a Bertelsmann company, focusing mainly on the call center out-sourcing operation's quality auditing. Mr. Han is involved in key account customer relations build up and maintenance and new project implementation. Before joining Arvato, he worked for Dell as an inside sales manager for three years and as a management trainee for BenQ for two years. He has experience in the tele-sales and call center operations (both on pre-sales and after-sales services), and he is certified as a COPC coordinator.

Chang Qing (Chris) Li (李常青) is an international business executive with a broad background of medical device design and manufacturing experience. He has held positions of senior process engineer, senior research and development engineer, and process engineering manager at Boston Scientific and is currently leading a start-up medical device company in China. Chris received a BS in chemical engineering from Tsinghua University in Beijing in 1995. Supported by a National Science Foundation scholarship, he was awarded a master's degree from the University of Akron in the same field in 1998. Chris earned his professional engineering license in 2000. In 2004, Chris received his MBA degree from the Kelly School of Business at Indiana University.

Wei Li is an international finance executive with seventeen years of experience in the technology industry. She currently serves as CFO for Sony Ericsson China. Prior to that, she worked with Dell China as a finance director. Before coming back to China and joining Dell, she had been working in the United States for years, associating with ioWave, NET-tel, and American Mobile Satellite Corp. as controller, finance manager. Wei Li is a graduate of Shanghai Jiao Tong University, with a BA in management. She holds an MA in accounting from American University and a CPA license from the University of Maryland. She received an MBA from the Wharton School, the University of Pennsylvania. She can be contacted at wei.li.wg03@wharton.upenn.edu.

Jun Liao is an experienced business manager at a Fortune 500 company. He has worked in various industries and across functional teams, ranging from advertising, design education, and operations management to marketing. With twelve-plus years of professional experience working in China and five years in the United States, he managed a team of one hundred employees and a business with $2 billion revenue. Mr. Liao is fluent in English and Mandarin. He holds an MBA from the University of Texas at Austin, and a bachelor's degree in engineering from Shanghai Jiao Tong University. He may be reached at junliao88@gmail.com.

Jiang Tao (Roger) Sun is the treasury manager at Starbucks, covering the greater China region. He has worked in the banking and treasury profession since he graduated from Nankeen University in 1994. Roger has also worked with Intel and Nestle and has broad exposure to various business projects that involve people from various cultures and business backgrounds. His work also requires interactions with bankers and government officials, in addition to internal business partners. Roger also holds a master's degree of applied finance from the University of Queensland, Brisbane, Australia. He can be contracted at roger.j.sun@ starbucks.com.

Julia Wu (吴珺) is in senior management in Worldwide Procurement of Dell Shanghai with experience in supply chain management, product engineering development, and product configuration management. She received a bachelor's degree of English literature from East China Normal University in Shanghai in 1994 and earned her MBA degree from ENPC Business School of International Management in France in 2007.

Dajun Yang received a master's degree in physical chemistry from Nankai University in 1997. He spent three years working at Proctor & Gamble as a researcher on the research and development team. In 2000, he started his career in sales/marketing. He worked as marketing engineer at ExxonMobil from 2000 to 2002. Then he joined Albemarle in 2002. Currently, he works in China as a catalyst sales manager in Albemarle. By working with customers like Sinopec and PetroChina in China refining and petrochemical industry, Mr. Yang has eight years of experience under two different cultures.

Jiahai (John) Zhang is originally from Jiayin Farm, Heilongjiang Province, in China. He currently lives in Honolulu, Hawaii, where he works as area coach for Panda Express. He has over eleven years of experience in the restaurant business and two years of experience in real estate. Frequently, you can find Mr. Zhang enjoying golf and basketball.

Zhen (Steve) Yang is a senior consultant at Deloitte Consulting in Shanghai China. He completed his MBA at the McCombs School of Business at the University of Texas at Austin in 2010. He has over six years of experience in the telecom industry and has served various positions in both multinational companies and start-ups. He earned a bachelor's degree from Shanghai Jiao Tong University and a master's degree from Concordia University in Canada, both in electrical engineering. He can be reached at steyang@deloitte.com.cn.

Quan (Michael) Zheng (郑权) is the partner of Beijing Biztravel International Travel Service Co., Ltd., which is an international travel company in China. With over sixteen years of experience in the travel industry, Michael has established a long-term and good business cooperation with the travel companies and institutions in the United States, Canada, Britain, Netherlands, Denmark, etc. His company received recognition for outstanding service during the 2008 Beijing Olympics Games. He graduated from Nankai University in 1991, the first university in China with a bachelor's degree in tourism.

ABOUT THE AUTHORS

Orlando R. Kelm, PhD, (University of California, Berkeley, 1989) is an associate professor of Hispanic linguistics at the University of Texas at Austin. His professional interests include teaching language and culture for professional purposes. His creative projects and publications focus on the creation of instructional materials, including the use of technology in foreign-language education. He currently serves as the associate director of business language education for the Center for International Business Education and Research at UT, Austin. For the past six years, he has led groups of UT MBA candidates to South America and China on business observation tours.

John N. Doggett, JD, (Yale Law School, 1972, and MBA, Harvard Business School, 1981) is an award-winning senior lecturer at the McCombs School of Business at the University of Texas at Austin. He is an ex-McKinsey consultant, former lawyer, and serial entrepreneur who has extensive business and consulting experience working with firms in Asia, Europe, and the United States. Since 2003, he has led business observation tours of MBAs to China and India and has worked with American, European, and Chinese executives on Chinese and American market entry issues. In the summer of 2005, he taught at the Chinese University of Hong Kong. He has been to thirteen cities in China and is married to Haiping Tang, a Chinese national who is the third author of this book.

Haiping Tang (MBA, McCombs School of Business, the University of Texas at Austin, 2000, and BA, English, Nankai University, Tianjin,

China, 1994) is a senior manager at Dell, Inc. She has extensive experience working with both Chinese and American managers in the United States, China, Taiwan, Hong Kong, and Singapore. She is married to John Doggett, an American who is the second author of this book.

9340479R0

Made in the USA
Charleston, SC
03 September 2011